ON THE ARIZONA ROAD

WITH BILL LEVERTON

words and pictures
by
Bill Leverton

The stories in this book are a compilation of stories done over the past 13 years by Bill Leverton. In some cases, the circumstances of the story may not have stayed the same. People may not be there any more, lives change, situations come and go.

The title "On the Arizona Road" is a copyright of KTSP-TV and Newscenter 10. Many of the chapters of this book were first shown on television and are the copyrighted property of KTSP-TV and Newscenter 10, who have kindly given permission for their use in this book.

Front cover artwork by Bruce Robert Fischer

Back cover photo by Bonnie Leverton

Library of Congress Cataloging-in-Publication Data

```
Leverton, Bill
   On the Arizona road with Bill Leverton.

   Includes index.
   1. Arizona--Social life and customs. 2. Interviews
Arizona.  3. Arizona--Biography.  I. Title.
F815.L47  1986           979.1           86-15015
ISBN 0-914846-26-4
```

Printed in the United States of America.

Golden West Publishers
4113 N. Longview Ave.
Phoenix, AZ 85014, USA

Dedication

This book and the motivation for all the years *On the Arizona Road* is dedicated to Ed Edgerton, who first started telling me the stories, and to Roman Malach, who took me to the high places.

God bless them. May they both rest in peace.

Contents

Sometimes it gets a little crazy. I'm taking a picture of Newscenter 10 photographer Jilliene Lutter taking a picture of famed photographer Josef Muench taking a picture of those two guys out on the ledge there. We were up on top of the Vermillion Cliffs north of the Colorado River.

In 23 years in television, I have been in front of more cameras in more places than you can imagine.

The road... why I'm out there!

It was late one frozen winter night on a highway in New Mexico when I almost got out of the news business. The wind snapped a snowy whip across the land, coming down out of the west, moaning and shrieking through the blackness. Stepping out of the news car that night I almost didn't go any farther. Snow stung my face, jammed up my nose, and I told myself I really hadn't seen anything.

It was a night back in the sixties when small-town television was young. We didn't have much money to do anything, and mostly we were given an old wind-up 16mm movie camera and carte blanche to shoot as many stories as we wanted on a hundred feet of black and white silent film. It was amazing how many stories I could get on a hundred feet. And mostly the stories were what I called the yukky, red-light-and-siren stories. We covered a lot of auto accidents and bank robberies and murders and armed robberies because we did that stuff really well.

Generally our instructions were to shoot pictures of every accident that involved injuries, and if we could beat the ambulance to the scene we became top reporters in the eyes of our news director. That's what I was doing that night. Not only had I beat the ambulance, I beat the state police car assigned the call, a car reported off the road about thirty miles west of Albuquerque.

It was just a quick reflection off to the side, something off in a lull in the driving snow. Flashlight in hand I literally fell down the embankment and damned near into the front seat of a car lying on its side, door open, windshield smashed, the smell of hot radiator water eddying on the freezing wind.

To make a long story short, I stumbled around and found an old man dying in the snow, thrown from the car. Kneeling down I ripped off my coat and threw it over him. He was trying to say something but the wind snatched away his words, scattered them out over the desert. He died.

Nothing graceful. Like in the movies, you know! He didn't just drift away... pass on... cross the great divide, stuff like that. This man died hard! With an ugly gasp and spouting of blood and a wild look in his eyes, he "passed on" violently. I had seen enough!

I am constantly impressed with the technology at our fingertips. The Arizona Road travels with portable microwave equipment to the top of one of the tall spires in Monument Valley. We sent live television pictures back to Phoenix. With me is engineer Ron Bradley (in shorts), photographer Evan Williams, and a Navajo lady who explained the legends of the valley to us.

And this is the monument we were on, Castle Rock. We were ferried in by helicopter.

I had come too close to it all. It's one thing to arrive at a scene and have all those who are going to die already dead and covered. It's another to participate. Just too much blood and guts. So I quit the news business. And promptly damned near starved.

To keep this long story still as short as possible, I wound up at KOOL-TV News, and somehow wrangled a deal where we started doing a thing called *On The Arizona Road.* Feature stuff, ghost towns, the Grand Canyon, people stories. I wouldn't have to cover the red-light-and-siren beat. Oh, occasionally, I had to, still have to, but not every day and every night and Sundays.

And that is what I've been doing for the past 10 of about 14 years at what is now KTSP-TV, Newscenter 10. Ten of the friendliest, most creative, most emotionally satisfying years of my career.

I get kidded a lot about my assignment. The "outhouse circuit" they say. "Take your camera and truck and go out into the hinterlands of Arizona and seek the outhouses. And do stories about people you find roundabout them." I don't guess anybody ever really said that, but it's a kinda loose translation of what my standing orders are.

So, I've done more stories in more ghost towns than I like to remember. Been on cattle drives, wagon trains, in towns too tough to die. Been up and down every wet and dry river in the state and talked to half the cowboys and cowgirls in the state and flown high and fast and gone low and slow and laughed . . . and cried . . . and covered more parades than anybody else I know except maybe Charles Kuralt (who, incidentally, is my idol). I had dinner with him one night and he told me that he considers himself CBS's "Master of the Irrelevant." Well, naturally, I started calling myself Arizona's "Master of the Irrelevant." Until too many people got to agreeing with me!

Another thing Charles Kuralt told me that night at dinner was that after we've discovered what all the makers and shakers are doing on the news . . . there doesn't seem to be anybody left. Except the folks. And having looked at the events of each day with some anger and not a little fear, it just seems OK to, every now and then, take a reassuring look at some part of life we can identify with. Maybe someone who lives out there some place where we can actually go and visit him if we have a mind to.

When you look there are some awfully neat stories out there . . .

A gentle man in a violent town

The men stood six feet apart in a dusty lot near the OK corral. They didn't like each other, and what was to happen had been a long time coming and it would be the beginning of several months of incredible violence. More than a dozen men would eventually die at the business end of a firearm.

It was a windy afternoon in October 1881. There are several versions of who started shooting first after those few frozen heartbeats when time stood still and an awful silence hung in the charged air. But just suddenly the day was shattered by explosions of gunfire. In half a minute, more than 30 shots were fired, the men blasting away at each other at close range.

The *Tombstone Nugget,* in its edition the following day, reported, "This day will always be marked as one of the crimson days in the annals of Tombstone. The day when blood flowed as water, and human life was held as a shuttle-cock." The *Tombstone Epitaph* wrote, "THREE MEN HURLED INTO ETERNITY IN THE DURATION OF A MOMENT!"

A hundred years later now. And darn it, I always forget to bring my boots when I come to Tombstone . . . The Town Too Tough To Die. I sort of envy the folks that walk the boardwalks of Allen Street in their Tony Lamas. The clomp-clomp-clomp their boots make on boards have just the right resonance here. Allen Street has been carefully maintained to look like things did a hundred years ago, and footsteps of other men . . . lean men with hard eyes and six guns . . . echo in the subconscious. There is just the right subliminal hint of violence, of OLD WEST. A rinky-tink piano is playing behind the swinging doors of a saloon. There is a flavor here, a musty violence that the Chamber of Commerce does its best to perpetuate. And I love it.

So, Tombstone is a town with a thousand violent stories. Not many towns in the old west could claim such stuff that movies are made of . . . such an intoxicating, turbulent atmosphere. Which means you'll probably miss the less violent stories. Such as the story of Pete Acuna.

The Wagon Wheel Bar and Restaurant isn't on Allen Street, it's over on the main highway through town. But it, too, has the old west look. Swinging doors, wooden floors, rustic furniture. But the music spilling out the swinging doors and into the night doesn't have the rinky-tink sound you'd expect. What you hear is an electronic organ playing an upbeat Harry James Big Band tune. A brassy saxophone cuts in. You peer over the swinging doors into a smoky saloon. A lot of cowboy-looking folks bellied up to the bar drinking Coors. Over in the corner is Pete Acuna, playing the sax AND the organ.

Pete Acuna plays the organ and saxophone AND the clarinet here at the Wagon Wheel Bar every Thursday through Saturday night. Pete Acuna is one of life's enigmas.

Now a Ranchera. The sound of Mexico . . . brassy but smooth. Sax with a mellow organ counterpoint, high stepping beat . . .

With all that's happened to him, Pete Acuna, almost fifty years old now, shouldn't even be alive. He had a heart attack a few years ago, and was blind from birth. He once weighed over three hundred pounds. He's still a little round, but nowhere three hundred pounds. The only thing that gave him any direction at all in his life was his music, which he began to learn at age six in a school for the blind. A couple of years ago he underwent surgery on his left eye, a radical new cornea transplant procedure.

Malagueña. Pete Acuna is singing Malagueña. His voice is high and sad and lonesome . . .

When they removed the bandages, Pete Acuna . . . could see! Do you hear me? After fifty years of darkness . . . he could see!

Not 20-20 vision, but he could see! He saw his wife for the first time, his friends. He saw the world around him.

"I was lookin' over and asking what this was and what that was and what the other was. Like . . . like those little white lines going the other way right down the middle of the road, you know? I was looking around from side to side, I guess, at the roads and the mountains and the sky. I was fascinated by it all . . . wanted to take it all in in one day."

He's playing all three at the same time now. The sax in one side of his mouth, the clarinet in the other, the organ with one hand. Neat, brassy, piercing music. Harry James again. Now just the sax. Then the clarinet. Nimble fingers race to the keyboard, then back to both horns again . . .

"I was just like a little kid on Christmas morning." Pete Acuna still has the mannerisms of a blind man, head cocked to the side, listening. But . . . he can SEE! "I . . . I don't know . . . I guess I haven't seen anything I've disliked yet." He thinks for a second. "Except the way some of these idiots drive around town."

Late now. Pete's singing Blue Bayou, slow, sad. Pete knows slow and sad. Folks dancing up close . . .

As Pete Acuna learns to see, his other senses seem to lessen. His hearing doesn't seem to be as sharp as it was, or his touch. People are saying to him . . . hey, Pete, you oughta hit the big-time with all your talent. But . . . he's pretty happy where he's at. This is where it's all been good for him. When he couldn't see. And now that he can.

So, this is one of the stories in Tombstone, Arizona. The Town Too Tough To Die. An easy story to miss. A gentle man in a town impressed with its violent past.

* * *

I went back to see Pete. I always go back. Sometimes I'm sorry I do. Sometimes the memory of the way things were, the nice way they seemed to turn out, would have been best. Things didn't turn out too well for Pete.

It was an accident, of course. Whoever did it is sick with remorse. Someone bumped into Pete, bumped him hard, hit him on the head. Tore the delicate mechanisms that had been repaired in his eye. Tore away, in an instant, what precious little eyesight Pete had. They aren't sure if the damage is repairable.

And Pete Acuna returned to the darkness of all those years.

I almost couldn't handle it, talking to him about this incredible misfortune. Pete had just finished playing a request for me, C-Jam Boogie. Lordy, how he plays that! He'd kill 'em down on Bourbon Street.

"Ah, Bill, I'm doing fine, just fine. I just have to be philosophical about it. I'm OK."

He plays his music. No more little white lines going the other way right down the middle of the road, you know. No more roads and mountains and sky. He plays his music . . . and we dance to his music . . .

Music we don't ever pay enough for.

Mystic maze

Up on a broad, sloping mesa overlooking the west bank of the Colorado River, and just into California off Interstate 40, the place is called the Mystic Maze.

It has been here for centuries, and all the bad ghosts and ugly spirits and hazy travelers of nether-worlds have been here, too. Floating about, trying to find a way out of the maze and into the land of the Mohaves. I arrived here late one windy afternoon in February to shoot a story about the place.

I was told that this was a place where long-ago Mohave Indians dealt with wandering spirits who had nefarious intent on the spiritual well-being of Indians' lives. The Mohaves laid out parallel windrows of rock several feet apart and about a foot high that weaved and curved across the mesa. The rows ran in many different diirections, some ending up against other rows, but generally they all wound up pointing northward.

The purpose of the maze was simple and practical. It was a way to cleanse the mortal, living Mohave Indian of unpleasant and evil, non-mortal spirits when he returned from trips outside his homeland.

The Mohaves were great runners and known to cover over 100 miles a day when traveling. Running over to the coast to trade with Indians there was not unusual. But, of course, wandering around outside the homeplace was fraught with dangers, not the least of which was exposure to unknown numbers of strange, unwanted and unfriendly spirits.

So, when they returned home, the Mohave reasoned that a swift run through the maze confused and lost all the evil spirits that might have attached themselves to the runner along the way, spirits hoping for a free ride down into the villages of the Mohave, where they could then jump off and wreak spiritual havoc among the people.

But the Mohave's villages were sacred and no bad spirits were allowed. Spirits and ghosts and emissaries of bad gods all fell by the wayside somewhere in the maze, lost, confused, unable to find their way out. Condemned to wander, brooding and sulking and kicking at things, through centuries-long tantrums.

The windrows of rock generally point toward a faraway peak which was known to be a great influence in Mohave spiritual matters. And the Needles Peaks just across the river also played an important role. The souls of Mohaves who died swung back and forth between the sharp peaks for four days until they gathered enough momentum to catapult them into the Other-World. But before the soul went to the peaks it, too, passed through the maze, this time to cleanse itself of earthly entanglements.

Before it was discovered and understood for what it was, about eight acres of the maze were destroyed when they built Interstate 40. Some ten acres remain today.

I'm finished filming, pack up. I stand in a spooky place, all by myself. A place where only the wind comes anymore, playing a lonely tune my imagination dances to. Shadows grow long in a fading day and ever so faintly running footsteps approach out of a corner of my mind. Suddenly I realize I've been wading around all afternoon among all those evil spirits shed by all those long ago Mohaves. The place must be absolutely thick with mean, evil specters and wraiths all just clawing to piggy-back a ride out of this maze, where the winds of endless years tumble them around, trapped and screaming and howling, tricked by mere mortals.

The land of the Mohave grows dark around me, and here on this lonely mesa bad spirits are about. It is time for me to leave. And hope I'm not taking some of them with me.

U.S. Government loses at Theba School

December 1977

Theba, Arizona, is one of those places along the road you'd miss even if you didn't blink. It's not even on the main road, really, it's on the access road to I-8 a few miles west of Gila Bend. Not a very big place, cotton growing country . . . out in the middle of nowhere. Two kinds of weather: warm in the winter, hot in the summer.

It would hardly seem an appropriate place to push a civil rights issue, especially when there wasn't even one to be pushed. But the U.S. Government landed on Theba in a big way.

Turns out, a lot of places ought to take a course from Tom Goyer on how to handle the U.S. Government.

There is a four-room, sixty-student school there alongside the interstate that operated on a budget of $190,000, all from local taxes. This is cotton country, remember, the tax-base is substantial. Fact is, some years they don't even collect all the taxes because they don't need them.

Well, seems this lady from Washington called Tom Goyer, the principal and the sixth, seventh and eighth grade teacher, and told him he was going to have to sign a pledge proclaiming he would not discriminate against women. A requirement, she informed him, for receiving federal aid. Make sure he would hire a proportionate number of women, stuff like that.

Goyer told the lady, we don't discriminate against women. And besides that, we don't get federal funds, and we aren't going to sign any paper.

The federal lady got testy, told Goyer they would cut off his federal money.

Ma'am, Goyer replied, listen to what I'm saying, we don't get any federal money.

OF COURSE YOU GET FEDERAL MONEY!!! screamed the lady from Washington.

All of which should have been a premonition of things to come for Tom Goyer and his little four-room school located in the heart of cotton country out on the desert west of Gila Bend.

The only men on the seven-person staff at the school were Goyer himself and Fernando Hernandez, who was the custodian, maintenance man and school bus driver.

"Yes, I'm fairly firm in this. And, uh, I've checked with the State Education Department and they say, stick in there." Tom Goyer talking. "There's nothing to comply with. It's all nonsense. I don't see filling out a form about civil rights. I don't see how that's going to help my kids here get educated. I don't see how it's going to help my teachers here be treated any better. I treat them as well as I know how now . . ."

Well, Goyer received a NOTICE OF COMPLIANCE in a proceeding in this case . . . the government wanted to know why he wouldn't sign that pledge, especially since he was at least eligible for federal aid.

"We ARE eligible to receive some kind of federal aid to education. But the last time this was checked out, we were eligible for ninety some dollars. For the whole year." Goyer laughs, "And once before that it was checked and we were eligible for twelve dollars . . ."

The hearing was set for January 1978, in San Francisco. Tom Goyer didn't go. And all that government paperwork was thrown in the trash can.

We couldn't help but notice the penalty for non-compliance in this whole matter. Pretty severe. The government warned Goyer . . . sternly . . . you guessed it . . . no more federal money!

*   *   *

I've always wanted to stop at the Theba School every time I pass that way and see if anything else ever happened. But guess I'm just a little afraid to. I have this nasty feeling the U.S. Government got to Tom Goyer. Somehow. Someway.

Roman Malach passes on

The only problem with traveling the Arizona Road is: sometimes the good friends you make pass on. It's hard not to get close to some of the folks out there, and that's why, as I sit here and work at this story, a great deal of sadness washes over me as I relive a lot of memories. A lot of memories about a good friend of mine, Roman Malach. Roman passed away Wednesday, December 4, 1985.

I had followed Roman Malach around the lonesome places of Mohave County ever since he was a young man of 70. He was 81, and still did a respectable job of hiking me right into the ground. I'll never forget the first day I met him. We were seated across the table from each other and he was telling me about some historical something and my attention wandered to a row of pictures on the wall behind him. WHAM!

Roman's hand slammed down on the table! Pencils, coffee cups and I leaped in the air, hovered for a micro-second, then fell back. My heart!

"YOU MUST PAY ATTENTION TO ME!" Roman never talked to anyone about anything that he didn't talk in capital letters. Meekly I replied, yessir. I didn't know it then, but Roman Malach spent most of his life teaching in the Continental United States and Alaska and I wound up on the receiving end of one of his best student-pay-attention-getters. Roman never, never made small talk and expected you to either be interested, or go away.

And I guess because I didn't get up and walk out in a huff on that day, Roman seemed to like me and I liked him and we became good friends and we did some neat things together.

For a number of years Roman was the Mohave County Historian, unpaid, un-heralded, sometimes a little too brusque, but a guy who, along with his wife, Doreen, traipsed all over the wilds of the county, stalking the elusive shadows of history.

Roman Malach was as colorful as the history he researched. He was born in the Empire of Austria, in an area now a part of Russia, and graduated from the University of Lemberg in 1926. He spoke six languages. When he came to the United States his family was

trapped behind by German occupation. His accent was still very strong . . .

"Mother died of starvation in the Nazi oppression." Roman was sitting in the shade of a boulder along an old wagon road that runs through the city limits of Kingman. It was impressively hot and the mid-day sun beat down out of a cloudless sky. We had been exploring the 100-year-old traces of this wagon road, a route wagon trains took across this part of Arizona in the 1800's.

"And at the same time I was told that my sister was hit in the head by a piece of shrapnel and became blind and died of those injuries. And my brother . . . no one exactly has facts . . . but he was kidnapped by force by Nazi people."

Roman taught school when he came to this country. During World War II he went to India with the Red Cross. He couldn't get into our armed services, but he desperately wanted to participate, in some way, in the fight against Hitler.

In 1971, retired, he moved to Kingman. He volunteered to do historical research for Mohave County. In his own inimitable style, writing like he talks, he produced over 30 small books about various aspects of the county's colorful mining history. Over the years, Roman Malach and I did stories for television about more old mines and more old wagon roads and more old sheriffs and more old 100-year-old mysteries than I can shake a stick at.

Roman Malach was a rotund man who barged ahead up and down steep slopes and off into rocky places and faraway places with all the determination of a man, say, like me, forty years his junior. Well, maybe not exactly like me. He wore me out a couple of times. History, according to what Roman Malach discovered, has many ramifications . . .

We were at Hackberry, for instance, a turn-of-the-century mining town just off old U.S. 66 east of Kingman. They were putting in one of those big electrical transmission lines across the valley there and an archeologist was sent to make sure no significant old ruins would be disturbed.

At a spot up above Hackberry, there is a ruin of something. Some old foundations, a garbage dump that looked like it might have been the scene of a turn-of-the-century beer party. Was it important? They turned to historian Roman Malach.

"The old-timers here explain that it was Bill Conway, local saloonkeeper, who built this . . . well . . . for local needs . . . or his needs . . . and it served the people here." Roman nodded his head as if to say, there, now you understand. Well, I was pretty sure I understood, but I liked to prod him every now and then . . .

"You're dancin' around here, Roman. What, exactly, was this?"

"Well, again I'm saying that he built this place with all his finances and used this for . . . the term was . . . used for . . . ladies of the evening!"

I laughed. Roman sure danced around. He grinned.

"Well, what else do you want?"

"That this . . .?"

"This is an historical place!"

Having this "historical" significance, this ruin hadn't, at the time, been disturbed.

Later, Roman Malach was no longer the Mohave County Historian. Until he died he did volunteer work for the Kingman field office of the Bureau of Land Management. But I had to wonder why he spent his retirement traipsing around the mountains and deserts of Mohave County, in the heat and the cold, for no pay whatsoever?

"Yes, that is as I sometimes say to people, a corny expression, that I am in small way repaying for the benefits of the life received here in this country because I would be dead long, long time, as every member of my family.

"You say that I am living in a good country. NO! That's not the word. You are living in a paradise country for me! It's a paradise! I never could dream that I could reach anything of material or any other values in life, even if I was there a Professor of University. I would be SLAVE!"

His voice rose, his hand waved in the air. "I WOULD BE SLAVE OF MY WORDS . . . SLAVE OF MY SPIRIT . . . SLAVE OF MY HEART! SLAVE!"

He slapped his knee and looked at me. "Anything else to add to it? No."

Crusty, loud, obstinate, searcher of lost history. That was my good friend, Roman Malach. We went to the high places and the lonely places and hunted for a sense of the way things were. He was a good friend of mine, and a good friend of Newscenter 10. I have to tell you . . . I loved this gruff old guy.

Please God . . . rest his soul.

Strange creatures
on the Arizona Road

It almost looks like Michael Morales, the head of the Department of Geology at the Museum of Northern Arizona, is playing a game of hopscotch, or mother-may-I, and he just got permission to take a bunch of giant steps. His exaggerated leaps across the desert floor near the Hopi village of Moenkopi are actually to give my television camera some idea of how far apart the footprints are. The footprints in the rock. The footprints from so long ago . . .

If you listen to some of the things Mike Morales has to say about the footprints, it's just gotta blow you away. He's talking about the footprints of a creature that lived 200,000,000 years ago. That's TWO HUNDRED MILLION years ago. And they lived right here in Arizona. And their species lasted a long, long time, about 140,000,000 years. That's ONE HUNDRED FORTY MILLION years.

We're talking about dinosaurs. They were anywhere from the size of a chicken all the way up to a lumbering beast that might have weighed 100 tons. They roamed Arizona in an age that was something we wouldn't recognize: swampy, wet, a time of receding seas; it would be millions and millions of years before flowers would bloom, before birds would fly.

The dinosaurs were plant eaters . . . and meat eaters. The meat eaters ate the plant eaters. In the area of the petrified forest there were monsters the size of a greyhound bus. Always hungry, always on the prowl for some tasty morsel that they could overwhelm or outrun or outsmart.

Just this summer, a little north from there, up in the painted desert, they discovered the bones of Phytosaur. About the size of a large dog, and maybe rather stupid, "Gertie" as he, or she, is being called, is "possibly the world's oldest datable, articulated dinosaur." Gertie lived 225 million years ago.

Over on the Navajo and Hopi reservations they've got more than just bones. They have footprints. Tracks of a beast that loped by 200 million years ago. This was Dilophosaurus. a meat eater who

Michael Morales dusts dinosaur prints

grew to about ten-feet long. And that brings us back to Mike Morales.

"And it was taking six-foot-long or so strides." Mike pointed down at distinct tracks in the hard sandstone rock, tracks about a foot long and a third as wide. "So he was running relatively fast, even for its size . . . about fifteen miles an hour. A four-minute mile. Now, look here, we have another track that crosses it . . ."

A total of twelve tracks trail across this ledge overlooking a Hopi cornfield. Enough tracks to establish what scientists call a "trackway." Enough tracks to determine how big the animal was that made them and about how fast he was moving.

"There were two of these guys, running together, sort of as a team, maybe, after some prey item which was going in this direction. That's one possibility. Another is that one was running after the other one." Mike raises his eyebrows and smiles . . .

The tracks at Moenkopi are not accessible to visitors. But more impressive, a veritable barn dance of dinosaurs, is a place where visitors can go, just off U.S. 160 west of Tuba City. Here, on some muddy afternoon longer ago than it's easy to imagine, one or two or a whole bunch of dilophosaurus stomped around hither and thither leaving all sorts of footprints . . .

"This footprint is about, oh, almost a foot in maximum length, from the tip of the middle toe to the back of the heel. And it shows really clearly claw impressions at the end of each of its three toes.

"At the time these tracks were deposited this was probably a relatively flat area, wetter than it is now, with nearby streams and rivers. It had probably rained and water had collected here, then started to dry up. Dinosaurs came down to drink water, and they walked on the mud, left their footprints. These footprints are all from about a day's time."

A day. One day in all the days of 140 million years of dinosaurs. A micro-blink across the eye of time. Then the day was over, and 200 million years went by. And the tracks remained.

"And the animal was probably six feet high at the hip-socket. Much bigger than the average man."

"And probably not a very even-tempered kind of creature," I mused.

Mike laughed. "No, probably rather aggressive. Huh, you've seen Hollywood productions of huge dinosaurs ripping up things in these movies . . . they probably acted a lot like that. Yeah, I think they might have."

Tracks. Tracks of a species that lasted 140 million years, then . . . just disappeared.

Tracks. Just enough to tickle our imagination, frustrate us with images of a lumbering beast that would have scared us silly had he come thundering toward us out of some misty place . . . from so long, long ago.

The last gunfighters

Two men tippy-toed slowly toward the door, guns drawn. The first man looked back at his partner, nodded. Then, turning back, he rushed the door, crashed through, leveling his pistol. He was way too late.

The outlaw inside fired the shotgun at point-blank range into the man plunging through the door, knocking him violently back into the street. The second man charged in, fired a shot, but the shotgun roared again. Outside, a dozen deputies scattered for cover.

Screaming, the outlaw dropped the shotgun, drew a pistol in each hand and ran crazily out the door, firing rapidly in all directions. A hail of lead from the deputies greeted him, lifting him up with each impact, punching him back into the wall of the building. Slumping down the wall, the outlaw fell over sideways on the boardwalk, dead.

* * *

Well, it was one violent afternoon when I met Duke Clark, the outlaw. We were shooting a documentary and Duke and the Oatman Gunfighters helped us dramatize one of the stories we were telling. Duke's been a friend of mine ever since and I've watched him put on more "old west gunfight" shenanigans than any one guy ought to be able to get away with.

Another afternoon in Oatman. Two ol' boys obviously in their cups have hit town to have a few drinks and they're kind of weaving down the street toward the saloon. One of them has saddlebags slung over his shoulder.

A hard-case steps into the street and confronts them.

"Hey there, boys!"

"Yeah?"

"Hear you got about $10,000 worth of gold in them thar bags!"

One ol' boy shifts a bleary eye toward the other. "We ain't got no gold."

(To make a long story short, everybody is convinced there is a lot of gold in the saddlebags. One bad guy after another appears and

Duke Clark

they all shoot each other trying to get at the saddlebags. Finally, with bodies strewn all over the street, the only ones left standing are the two good ol' boys with their saddlebags.)

Good ol' boy #1, standing unsteadily amidst all the bodies: "We told you guys they ain't no gold!"

Good ol' boy #2: "Thas' right. There ain't no gold!"

Good ol' boy #1 opens the saddlebags, reaches in. "We just come to town to have fun!" His hand comes out full of candy that he throws to the kids in the Saturday afternoon crowd lining Oatman's boardwalks. The crowd laughs, applauds. All the dead bodies get up and take a bow.

Oatman is an old mining town west of Kingman that kind of relaxes in its memories and treats tourists nice and has a lot of burros roaming the streets and you're just as likely to catch ol' Duke giving you the bad eye around some corner as not.

But it's a practiced, theatrical bad eye, part of the flavor of this town he's been a bad guy in . . . and a good guy and a drunk and a sheriff and a lout and more characters than he can remember . . . for the past 14 years. He's been "killed" more times than he likes to think about, and if he had really "killed" everybody he's dropped with blanks, he would go down in history as the world's most prolific killer. I like to think of him and his friends as sort of, well, the last gunfighters.

When they aren't out putting on one of two shows they do every Saturday and Sunday, most of the Oatman Gunfighters can be found in the saloon. One or two of them might be tearing up the dance floor with some of the female tourists passing through town. A sign over the bar says, DRINKING IS A GOOD WAY TO FIND OUT IF YOUR NECK LEAKS."

"We enjoy entertaining people." Duke himself doesn't drink much more than water these days. Stomach problems. "And it's kinda' nice to go down to the local grocery story and have the little kids look at you in awe. You know? It's all part of it."

Duke laughs. "There's a lot of times I'd rather take a beating than go out there. But once I get out there, I don't see anything but what I'm doing. I don't see the people or anything else. What I'm doing is what I'm doing. And I usually get into the role real well. I like it."

The cowboy walks up, pats Belle on the shoulder as he walks by. "Hello, Belle."

Duke shoots him dead. Belle clickety-clacks over to Duke on high heels. "I WISH YOU'D STOP DOING THAT, YOU CRAZY . . .!"

"But, you're my girl, Belle, an' he was fooling around with you . . ."

"I AIN'T YOUR GIRL . . . YOU'RE CRAZY! HE WAS JUST SAYING HELLO! LOOK WHAT YOU'VE DONE!"

The street is carpeted with "dead" cowboys, all of whom have touched Belle in some way or the other. Brushed against her, shook her hand, handed her something. Duke is a jealous cowboy. The skit is hilarious and the crowd laughs and laughs. Duke finally gets his. Belle gets his gun away from him and, well, you can figure out the rest.

Ah, there is an endless fascination to the old west. There's just something about the way those guys back then lived their lives . . . or the way we PERCEIVE they lived their lives that has a romance all its own. Of course, the best part is always the most violent part.

So, these days we still have a bunch of grown men who wear their pistols full of blanks low on their hips, come out and squint steely-eyed down a bunch of dusty western streets and "kill" each other regularly. They are the last of the gunfighters.

Duke sips his water. Straight. On the rocks. "In order to put on these type of performances you have to totally absorb yourself in the role in order to come out with a good performance. And so we

actually become these people for these short spans of time."

But in Oatman the Weekend Gunfighters face a far more serious threat than the business end of a Colt .45. The town is usually overrun with burros that come down out of the hills and wander the streets and sidewalks, begging handouts. You can imagine what the problem is . . .

"We used to have one gunfighter, he got so leery about that that he was ruining every gunfight. 'Cause he kept looking in back of him to see if there was a pile of stuff he might fall in. And he usually did. He's gone!"

All the gunfighters along the bar laugh at the memory of the gunfighter who was more afraid of donkey droppings than anything else.

Long shadows run away the sun. The tourists go wherever tourists go. The burros wander off. The band in the saloon (three guys: a drummer, steel guitar and electric guitar player) plays one last tune. One of the gunfighters dances with a lady in a wheelchair. Gently rolls her wheelchair around and around the dance floor, does a shuffling two-step. A last splash of fading sun back-lights the woman's face. She's smiling. Nobody asked him to do that, nobody told him to do that. He's just a nice guy. They all are and I'm proud to know 'em. The last of the gunfighters.

The 1948 Buick transmission torque converter blues

(in metal flat minor)

The barber shop was just a little place, located where you'd really have to look for it if you hadn't been there before. I had to look for it. It was on the back side of the shopping center, around where mostly you find the back doors of the places up in front. Not a fancy place either, no sissy stuff. No washes or perms, just a plain old haircut. A place to get the ol' ears lowered, maybe a shave, catch up on the gossip. For about half the price of those other places.

It was Hiram Gilbert's barber shop back in '78 when I did the story. Hiram Gilbert was 57 then, and had been a barber ever since he was 14 years old. He readily admitted it hadn't been all haircuts and shaves and, since he didn't do any of that sissy stuff, he'd had some time on his hands. So, among a few other things he'd done to keep himself occupied, he learned to play a banjo. Then he learned to make banjos. Then he did something weird. He started making his banjos out of, of all things, 1948 Buick transmission torque converters.

He what? "At one time, I, uh, heard some guy that built one out of a '48 Buick and, well, not the whole Buick, just the torque converter, you know, and I checked into it and I just, uh, got started."

Three 1948 Buick torque converters later now. "And the part, the converter, well, it works out pretty good, I think." He laughed. "Someone remarked to me once it might even work better as a banjo.

"Now this ring inside . . . that's the most important part, the thing that does the trick. It acts as a tone ring, a sound ring . . ."

He dragged over a chair and propped his right foot up on it, strummed the banjo strings, made a couple of adjustments, head cocked to one side, listening. His fingers began to strum out a tune. Couple of mistakes at first, but gathering confidence, medium beat, kinda pretty.

"I been workin' on this one. Gonna call it my own personal blues." He chuckled, missed a string. "The Hiram Gilbert 1948 Buick Transmission Torque Converter Blues."

A few more bars . . .

"Yep, I think it'll work."

The finished product looks and acts like the real thing. It perhaps glistens with a bit more metallic gleam than it should, but any casual observer would be hard-pressed, and surprised, to discover there was a 1948 Buick torque converter in there, much less a few other miscellaneous parts from the same car. A part of the bumper here, a little chrome there, some rings and things.

A true student of music complete with discriminating ear might scoff here, but he wouldn't scoff long. The music, over the years, has sounded pretty good to Hiram Gilbert, and to his friends. And they are all folks big enough to kick you out on your duff if thee scoffs too much. It is, after all, what sounds good that matters.

Hiram Gilbert has made three of these banjos, that's all the 1948 Buick torque converters he's been able to find so far. But the search goes on. There are slack times in the barbering business, you know, and his banjos are not for sale, don't call and ask. They are his pleasure, his own personal escape from what we all feel from time to time . . . that old eight to five drudgery. You don't sell your escape.

A few more bars, then someone wandered in looking to get the ol' ears lowered . . .

That ol' Hiram Gilbert 1948 Buick transmission torque converter blues, hummmm . . .

The waver

Seven thirty in the morning, 57th Avenue and Campbell. Out of all the people who will pass this corner on this muggy day in August a whole bunch of them will definitely expect to see . . . 74-year-old Perry Huskinson.

Perry Huskinson will wave at them. They will wave back. That will complete what has become, over the past year, a daily morning and afternoon ritual at this Phoenix intersection, a friendly wave.

Perry Huskinson wears a straw cowboy hat, he's average height, average looking, maybe a little overweight.

"Was takin' a morning walk before breakfast to pick up my newspaper . . . HELLO," Perry waves at a teenaged girl and boy driving by in a souped-up Ford. They wave back. "Paperboy kinda went haywire on me . . . an' wanted to exercise, ya know . . . HEY, 'LO!" Little old lady heading south. She smiles and waves. "So, well, I been living here around 25 years, ya know, an' I was seeing a lot of my friends going to work . . . wave at 'em. Ya know."

"HELLO!" A nurse in a beige Pinto, motoring west. Surprised, but she waves.

Perry Huskinson not only waves at his some 300 regulars every day, he waves at everybody. Not everybody waves back. Guy in a pickup turning south off of Campbell. Perry smiles and waves. Guy stares, frowns, staring into the sun. Shields his eyes with his right hand to get a better look, gets a funny look on his face, you can almost hear him thinking, "Who is that old fool, anyway?"

Doesn't matter, though, the "old fool" still waves. And smiles.

Rain or shine, he is here, every day, Saturdays, Sundays and holidays. Life swirls around him. Fire truck speeding south, siren wailing, air horn blasting, red lights winking, roars past Perry in a tornado of dust and swirling paper from the gutter. Perry waves.

The fireman bouncing along on the back of the truck waves back.

Six to eight in the morning and three to five in the afternoon. An island of amiableness along a river of human detachment. Windows rolled up, temperature-controlled capsules carrying creatures temporarily afraid of each other and each other's intentions, withdrawn in themselves until they arrive at their destination where once again they step out and maybe say . . . hello.

To Perry Huskinson it only seems the friendly thing to do. And since he's been retired these last eight years, it also has become a kind of hobby, standing out and waving at all his friends.

He has a gruff voice . . . "I been goin' to church for years an' have lotta friends, ya' know . . . 'LO, HELLO!" Man in a business suit waves and hollers, "'LO, GUY!"

"I try to do some good if I can. One day there was a fella stop and get out of his car an' come over to me and wanted to thank me big 'cause I waved at him that morning. I just thought, I don't know what's hurtin' on his mind, but I might have helped him a whole lot . . ."

A very pretty lady stops at the light, next to the curb. Perry bends over and peers in the window, waves. "'LO, THERE!"

The pretty lady jerks her head toward Perry in surprise, looks a little frightened, then smiles and waves. Not a very big wave, but a wave. The light turns green and she drives off.

A lot of cars going by now. Perry waves with both hands at cars going every direction. People waving back. Brief smiles in a journey of detachment, a journey of careful neutrality. That's what Perry Huskinson looks for, the smiles, that's what makes it all worth it.

So you might say, they also serve who only stand and wave.

"...and you can't find my bags?"

I'm going to be honest about this. When this article is published I'm going to send a copy of it to the airlines. I know just an irate letter won't do any good. And, still being honest, this didn't happen *On The Arizona Road.* But, it started from the Arizona Road.

It was going to be a quick, pleasurable weekend, over to Albuquerque to visit friends, a little party. The party was scheduled to start three hours after I got to Albuquerque and it would take an hour to drive to where they live north of town. Even if the plane was late there would be plenty of time.

America West was right on time. Folks pouring out of Phoenix headed for a weekend of skiing in New Mexico or on up to the plane's second stop, Durango, Colorado. And one guy going to a party. I checked my suitcase.

I can only guess how many people got off at Albuquerque, but I think about 40. I picked up my car at Hertz. Perfect, things going like clockwork. I hurried over to the baggage carrousel. I recognized several of my fellow passengers, smiled, nodded. They didn't smile back. The carrousel was empty, rotating slowly, shiny.

Twenty minutes now since we got off the plane. One lady kept peering hopefully up the tube our luggage should come spilling out of.

Now we are all standing at the America West ticket counter, wanting to know where the hell our luggage is. The America West gal behind the counter is obviously not a supervisor or boss of anything. I get the impression somebody thought it was a good time for lunch.

"The luggage was overflown to Durango, folks. Everybody's." She smiled at us bravely. Not a smile in return. "Either that or it never got put on in Phoenix."

A collective, "What?!"

A guy, even younger than the gal, is at the counter now.

"What happened, see, the baggage handlers opened the compartment and all the Durango baggage was on top and they just assumed there wasn't any baggage for Albuquerque."

"You mean to tell me that just a few feet from them several dozen people are getting off the plane and they 'just assume' there's no baggage?" The passenger is incredulous.

"I've got a meeting in Santa Fe this afternoon. My suit's in there." Another passenger.

The guy hands a form to the passengers. "If you'll all just fill out this form . . ."

Several passengers are apoplectic. They've got us. In a world where technology can send men to the moon and back, something has failed at the most basic level and we simply cannot have our luggage. Somebody, in a fit of convoluted deduction, decided forty people hit town without any baggage.

"That plane'll be back from Durango in two hours with your luggage, folks," the gal announces. She turns away and I hear her mumble to the guy, "I hope."

The plane comes back in two hours and my luggage finally came tumbling onto the carrousel. I was way late for the party. But in spite of the baggage handlers at American West, who I figure knew I was going to this great party and were jealous and did everything they could to keep me from having a good time, I had a good time. But, and I can only marvel at this, it took me THREE times as long to get my bags as it did to get to Albuquerque.

There are a thousand baggage-horror stories out there. Another time America West lost my luggage and promised as soon as they found it they would deliver it to my home. At 2 a.m. the next morning my doorbell rang. I staggered sleepily to the door. There on the front porch sat my bag. The night was quiet, dark. They had dumped my bag, punched the doorbell and split.

My mother and father came out to visit for the summer. The airlines lost their bags, really lost them. My folks had to buy a whole new wardrobe. One month later, to the day, a guy comes to the door. "Here's your luggage," he announced cheerily. Turned and walked away.

Remember Flip Wilson, the comedian? One of his characters was fond of yelling at the guy behind the ticket counter, "YOU MEAN TO TELL ME YOU CAN FLY THAT PLANE 600 MILES IN THE DARK AND FIND LOS ANGELES . . . AND YOU CAN'T FIND MY BAGS?"

World's most married man
August 1979

Blythe, California that August afternoon was hot. Not just . . . hot, but HOT. On a shabby side street, there was a shabby hotel, run by a kind of shabby-looking guy by the name of Glynn "Scotty" Wolfe.

To gain entrance to the hotel you ring a buzzer and talk through a slot in the door to a mouth and part of a nose. If you pass inspection, the bolts slam back, the door scrapes open, and you're inside.

The air-conditioning doesn't work very well, the place is dark, lit by bare, hanging, low-wattage bulbs. The walls are covered with pinups from girly magazines. There are Polaroid shots and snapshots of other women, some dressed, some not, some with Scotty in them, all smiling. Scotty Wolfe offers me a hot dog and a Pepsi.

He is an unusual person, this Scotty Wolfe. Not because of this strange, run-down old hotel that doesn't seem to have any guests, but because, Scotty claims, he is the world's most married man.

Since his first marriage in 1927, the 72-year-old man has been married 23 times. Married to two women twice, married to one woman five years, to another only 26 days.

His life has brought him from the hotel business in Los Angeles, where he was reputedly a very well-to-do man, to this decaying hotel in Blythe where in January 1979, Scotty Wolfe filed for bankruptcy.

We are in the kitchen and I'm chewing on a hot dog and sipping Pepsi. Scotty's left hand is up, fingers out, ticking off a count. "Helen was the first. Marjorie next, 'bout the time that song came out in the twenties. Then Marjorie again . . ."

Apparently Scotty pays no alimony or child support. All the wives signed a PRE-nuptial agreement that took care of all the POST-nuptial disagreements.

"Mildred. Thelma. Mary. Peggy. Shirley."

I shake my head and munch at my hot dog, sip my Pepsi.

𝍤 𝍤 𝍤 𝍤
||||

"Cathy. Paulette."

Sometime in the next thirty days Scotty was to be married for the 24th time, this time to a woman from Rio de Janeiro.

"And my Ma, ya know, she's kinda funny. She tells me she feels like she's the mother-in-law of the whole town. Wanna 'nother dog there?"

I wave him off.

"Anyway," he's starting back over the same fingers, "Esther . . . Gloria. And, oh, let's see, Elizabeth, Lupita, Sherry. Then Maria-Victoria from Ecuador. And then I married her girlfriend Maria Chavez." This is where I lost track, lost the beat of women-past ticking by on his fingers. Why had he been married so many times?

"After you're married it gets to be the same old routine, kind of a drag around the hotel. And going places they get challenges and there's always guys after 'em. You dress 'em up and somebody wants to take 'em away from you. That's the game." He sniffs. "So I let 'em go. They wanna go . . . go!"

"Scotty, how many children do you have by all these marriages?"

𝍤 𝍤 𝍤 𝍤
𝍤 𝍤 𝍤 𝍤

"Got forty children on the record." He looks pleased with himself. I almost spit Pepsi in his face.

"Forty!" I gasp.

Scotty Wolfe is in the Guinness Book of Records for having the most monogamous marriages in the world. He has appeared on television and radio shows all over the world. He claims he is an ordained Baptist minister.

Almost giggling, I ask, "You ever have family reunions?" Of

course he doesn't.

"Yeah. Yeah, we have family reunions. Well, at least we used to have them. In Las Vegas. Well, it's been quite a while. About fifteen years, I guess. And, there might be six or seven come. But, they all eventually got married and their husbands get jealous, you know, and they won't go for that. And the kids get big and Momma don't always tell the kids what she did when she was young."

Somewhere in among the pinups and stuff on the walls there are pictures of all the wives. Smiling. Scotty's in there, too. Smiling. And there are fading newspaper articles dating back through the years. Back when he had only been married ten times. Or fifteen. Or twenty.

Scotty told me he was to marry his twenty-fourth bride, Regina Santos of Brazil, and the first woman over twenty he's married, on a TV show in Chicago.

He thought, he told me then, that marriage would last. But he admitted he's thought that all along.

I haven't been back. I hear he's been married a couple of times since that August afternoon in 1979.

Much ado about . . .

Nothing. A place along the road. Sort of . . .

Traffic speeds by on highway 93 heading to, or coming back from, Las Vegas. Next stop northbound from this spot is Wikieup, then Kingman. South an hour or so is Wickenburg.

At the top of the hill here, a wide spot in the road called "Nothing." A gas station for all outward appearances, but, subtly, something more than that. Only four people live at Nothing and the day I did the story half of the population was gone. They were off to a bigger town for a visit.

A high wind whistled out of the north and spun a half-dozen plastic propellers and wind vanes on the roof into a rattling, high rpm frenzy. One of the gadgets was a duck whose legs rotated in the wind. Let him hit the ground and he'd be in Kingman an hour before the rest of us.

You can buy gas, or a souvenir of your stay, here at Nothing. Best souvenir bet seems to be a t-shirt that says "When you've seen Nothing, you've seen everything." (I'm wearing my NOTHING shirt even as I write this.) On the back of the shirt is a plug for the Tain't Much Bar, which tain't much. (They probably stored tires and oil in the bar back in some dusty day when this was a serious gas station.) And I can tell you, tweren't much happening there the day I wandered in. Might say . . . NOTHING . . . was happening.

Also for sale are Tain't Much hats. But if you want the budget souvenir, go for the "rock concert," a collection of grungy old rocks pasted to a cardboard. Or a sack of nothing (an empty sack with the word "nothing" scrawled across the outside). Keith Wilkerson, one-fourth of the population of Nothing told me, "Sent one of them bags of nothing to President Reagan for Christmas. Din't hear nothin'." He laughs, looking over at Al Yount, another fourth of Nothing's population. Al laughs politely. He's heard this one a thousand times.

If you don't want to buy anything, and before Keith gets wound up and spouting nothing-isms, well, you can read the signs on the wall. One tries to drum up business for the Tain't Much Bar, "Some people will stop at Nothing for a drink," it says. Oh, and be careful

Keith Wilkerson (left) and Al Yount watch...nothing...go by

not to step on Smoky, the vicious guard dog lying in a warm, sun-induced coma beneath the sign. (Smoky is a black mongrel puppy that weighs all of three pounds).

Sometimes Keith and Al are busy here. But mostly not. A lot of the time they just kinda' stand around and watch the world speed by a hundred yards out on Highway 93. Semi's, shifting up after the long climb. Pickups, local ranchers. Cars, many headed to hit the jackpot in Vegas; others, pockets empty, headed back.

The day I was there a car drove in with a young couple. They stopped out about 150 feet from the station, sat there a full two minutes staring suspiciously at us. Ohio plates. We stared back. Finally the guy got out and snapped off a quick picture and leaped back in his car and threw it in reverse and screeched onto the blacktop heading south. His dust followed him on the wind.

Al Yount nods. "Yeah, that happens. Say, you think when they see me on your television program I could get a job in Hollywood?"

"Boy, I don't know," I answer.

It might have spooked those folks (well, this is "out west," you know), but this is a friendly place, and these are nice people. For instance, you don't have to buy anything to use the restroom. These days, that's friendly!

A lot of regulars up and down 93 stop in to shoot the breeze with Keith and Al. "Somebody comes in and says what's hap'nin'? And we say, 'nothin'. Whadda ya do 'round here for entertainment?' 'Nothin'." Keith laughs, looks at Al, who laughs politely.

Al is still thoughtful, "I just bet Hollywood is gonna wanna talk to me when they see me on television."

Now Keith laughs, politely. They've done these lines a million times before, but they're still, yeah, funny.

Keith's sister and brother-in-law bought the place and all their acquaintances and friends kept asking them, "Why'd you do that? What's up there?" Well, "Nothing," they answered, and they answered "nothing" so many times . . . well, you get the picture.

Two ladies on their way to Phoenix after a weekend in Las Vegas stop in for a soda pop. Keith has trouble getting into their sophisticated, computerized cash register. Actually it's a drawer that's been broken for so long that the only way it opens is to hit the top of the counter in just exactly the right place. WHAM! Then it flies open. Not a good idea to be standing in front of it.

Al points at me and tells the ladies, "I'm on my way to Hollywood."

Some people get confused when they arrive at Nothing.

"They all think they're nowhere, most people do." Keith laughs. Al laughs. Politely. "But they're not . . . Nowhere's over on the other highway." (There is a place called Nowhere just over the hills to the east, but after Nothing it can only be anticlimactic.)

I can only tell you . . . this has been a real nothing story.

I have to leave. "Well, uh, thanks for nothin', guys."

"Yeah, and that's just exactly whacha' got . . . nothin'!"

Little dealies up on the roof spin a rattling, windblown frenzy . . .

"Don't fergit nothing . . ."

Smoky, the vicious guard dog, hasn't moved the whole time. Only the rise and fall of his fat little tummy indicates he's even alive.

"Come back and see nothin' . . ."

Keith and Al laugh. I think they mean it this time.

"You got my address for when Hollywood wants to get me?" Al yells as I drive off. I wave.

If you come this way and you have . . . nothing . . . to do, stop at Nothing . . . and do nothing . . . with some real experts.

* * *

The other day I was on my way up to Kingman to do a story. I always like to visit folks I've done stories with. So when I came up on Nothing I pulled in, pulled up to the pumps. Al Yount wandered out and bent down to look in the window.

"Hi ya' there, Bill."

"Hey, Al, anything happening since I last saw you?"

"Nothin'."

Ed Edgerton

Ed's Camp is still there. It's not the same, of course. Nothing much ever does stay the same, especially after the spirit that moved it passes on. Ed Edgerton was the spirit, and the spirit died when he died, but his memory will always hang well on the walls of my mind.

On a warm spring morning in 1975 I drove out across the desert west of Kingman on old U.S. 66, exploring the road across the Black Mountains to Bullhead City. Somebody had told me I ought to see the old mining camp of Oatman, and the shambles of Gold Road, and the steep, rocky slopes where a grizzled old hard-rock dreamer by the name of Jose Gerez picked up a rock to throw at a stubborn burro. A rock, to Gerez's surprise, that had gold in it. And, in the best tradition of gold camp stories, the gold rush that followed produced millions of dollars in gold and silver. And millions of stories.

Old 66 had been abandoned to the modern, high-speed four lanes of Interstate 40 a few miles to the south. The two-lane highway that had once been the Mainstream of America was now pitted with suspension-killing chuckholes, the yellow dividing line was indistinct, and the possibility of traveling between Kingman and Oatman without ever seeing another soul was pretty good. If you did see another soul and he was driving toward you, passing became a severe test of depth perception in the narrow lanes.

Up off the desert floor, a twisting, winding snake of crumbly blacktop that eventually crossed a ridge of the Black Mountains at a place called Sitgreave's Pass. The desert pushed up in inhospitable and craggy high ridges, scrub brush, cactus, black rocks, bleak cliffs. Past the ruins of an old gas station, then suddenly into a pretty little canyon full of tall green trees, swaying gently in an easy breeze. Around a sharp curve, rattle across a rickety wood bridge, and there was Ed's Camp. And Ed.

Ed was leaning against one of those old, gravity-fed gas pumps the first time I saw him, nonchalantly, in a posed sort of way. I had the impression he might have heard me coming and rushed out into what was his "greet the folks" nonchalance. An impression, mind

you.

Not a very tall man, thin, eyes squinting against the sun, lots of laugh lines, and a sparkle there that was fueled by some inner humor. He walked from place to place a little bit hunched over and very fast.

Ed's Camp was hard to describe. It used to be a gas station and restaurant. But when traffic went south to the interstate, it gradually became a repository for a rambling collection of . . . well . . . stuff. Rusty stuff, parts of stuff, unidentifiable stuff, weird stuff. Old cars and trucks and boats and mysterious stuff. Stuff the uses for were lost in dust and rust and forgotten projects. But a pleasant enough place in spite of what we might, in haste, call junk. For me, it would become a magic place.

One thing that hadn't rusted over the years was Ed, who still hummed around puttering on this project, hammering on that one, busy, always busy.

Ed had spent nearly all his ninety years in the mining camps of this part of the state, and his memory was still sharp. He was often consulted about the history of the gold and silver mining camps that were in these hills.

Ed's Camp had been here for fifty years. And in those years tall trees had grown, an orchard had sprung up, and Ed had never given up the dream of making big money from the gold still left out there in the hills.

He was building a gold processing mill the first time I met him, was expecting to have it done soon. We walked over to his contraption, a real Rube Goldberg outfit. A large metal cylinder, rusted, big enough to sleep in with lots of gears and things sticking out . . .

"And you think that mill's going to do a number for you . . .?"

"That's gonna put me back on Easy Street." Ed pats the rusty monster affectionately. A splotch of rust comes away on his hand.

"So what're you gonna do when you're on Easy Street?"

Ed gazes off toward the hills. The ones with the gold in them. "I tell you! I like to gamble! I like to spend money! I like to get a kick outta that money!"

It was a good afternoon for listening to a story. Warm, pleasant.

"Ya know, years ago," he said, "I just blew in the money as fast as I made it. And the other fellows put it in the bank. And the banks went broke! They didn't get no good out of it! I did! Made a dozen fortunes mining, gambling, mining . . . went back, spent 'em! And go back and get some more. And I'll keep on doing that."

Ed brought his hands together in front of his chest, fingers together, stiff, straight, hands touching at the fingertips. He looked at his hands, then at me, eyes squinty in the spring sunlight. In a dramatic voice, "THE HANDS OF A GAMBLER!"

Leaves rustle softly in the tall trees, the only sound as Ed, hands still together, waits for a reaction. It is early in my career as the Arizona Road Reporter, and it is a turning point in my career. This is a place where you either start to believe . . . or you never will. You HAVE to believe. It doesn't matter if the story is stone-cold, affidavit true or not, not really . . . you just gotta believe.

I believed him.

But then Ed made some claims modern science will dispute. Or claims about some things modern science maybe doesn't know about yet. "I dried up cancer in my body in ninety hours. By use of high temperature, 135 degrees, with radioactive pads around me."

Now it was my turn to stare off at the hills. Uh . . . yeah.

"Excited by electrical pads. Yessir!" He thumped the fortune-making mill for emphasis. More rust fell away.

"I've outlived all the oldtimers in the district. None of the oldtimers are left. I'm the last of the bunch."

"How old are you?"

"Well, I'm closer to ninety than I am to eighty."

Closer to ninety than he is to eighty. Long years in the Oatman district. An old man who knew just about everything about what these hills had to hide, except maybe EXACTLY where it was hidden. He did discover a new metal one time. This IS a stone-cold fact. They called it Edgertonite for a while, but in the way of scientific lingo and the men who make it up, Edgertonite didn't sound scientific enough, or was too easy to pronounce, or something, so they changed it to something else. Sometimes, it seems, they just have to take away that one small honor that would mean so much . . .

* * *

I kept going back to Ed's Camp. I didn't always do stories, I just liked to wander around the place with Ed and listen to his stories about the district. We went up into the hills one day and peered down into black depths of old glory holes, scraped at rocks and dirt and sifted stuff through our fingers. "Still lots of gold out here," he'd cackle. "Used to be a big vein here, but it petered out." He rubbed his chin, thoughtfully. "I think I know where it might start up again. Gonna look for it one of these days."

Then we'd go back to his place and he would patiently explain to me, for the umpteenth time, how that gold processing mill worked. It always sounded to me like the "framus goes round and connects to the jinglerod to moderate the dizzle-sifter and the rock goes in here and the gold comes out there." The plans had been in the works for a long time.

And when we weren't talking gold we'd be over touring his orchard with its exotic experiments in cross-breeding of various fruits and nuts and trees and sweet-smelling stuff vining around on the ground. He had squash that came up to my waist when stood on end. And there were peaches and apples and strawberries and warm breezes and little bees buzzing in and out among the fragile pink and white blossoms and laughter.

Then one day in another spring, the spring of 1978, I went to sit and talk a while and I found Ed Edgerton gone. He was sick and in the Veterans' Hospital in Phoenix.

Later that week, when I returned to Phoenix, I found out his problem. Mostly just age, the creaking and groaning of old bones. He did, of course, tell the doctors what was wrong with him and what to do about it. The doctors did, of course, know better, and ignored him. And my feeling was, the day I went to visit, that the nurses were pretty well fed up with the old coot and told me curtly which room he was in and would I please leave them alone about him.

It occurred to me that there was something wrong here. There was no appreciation of this colorful old man. This short, skinny, kinda hunched old man who had lived most of his years in a life that makes most of ours seem a little dull. Maybe it's why we younger folks don't ever seem to have the patience to listen, because maybe we are afraid to hear that somebody has done things far more interesting in their lives than we have in ours. An old man in the hills, anchored there all his life by the unbreakable lure of dull, yellow rock. A fascination that kept men like Ed Edgerton dazzled all the years of their lives. They just knew . . . just knew in their hearts . . . there was more gold out there in the hills, just waiting for the right man to come along and take it.

To his dying day, Ed Edgerton believed he was that man. He always let me know he had, "the hands of a gambler."

Ed and his gold processing mill

So, standing there in the warm sun of what became a lonely spring afternoon, I felt a panicky thump in my heart. A loneliness whispered down through the breeze, magic slipped away. The orchard and garden were overgrown with weeds, the fence needed repair. Something that should have been nailed down slapped in the wind.

I came here on a warm spring afternoon to sit and talk a while with my friend Ed Edgerton.

He wasn't here.

In the story I did for television that day I said, "It's a lonely place here right now. It needs . . . well, that special touch that only you seem to have, Ed. So try and get well . . . and come on back."

He never got well. He did come back, nobody paid him much attention . . . and four months later he passed away.

He was gone.

He left still looking. Always he looked for that elusive color. And somehow it always eluded him. At least in the big, grand, glorious way he would like to have found it.

Funeral services were simple and short. A handful of people, a few oldtimers.

And echoes of the man raced through my mind. Remembered words . . .

"I've outlived all the oldtimers in the district. None of the oldtimers are left. I'm the last of the bunch!"

The last of the bunch.

I cried like a baby.

Ed Edgerton was cremated. Someone told me he wanted to have his ashes spread over his place. So I rented an airplane and flew up over Ed's Camp. Made two passes. Threw out his ashes on the first. Came in low the second time and wiggled the wings in salute. Ed would have considered it pretty good drama.

In that last story I stood in front of the creaky old gate that opened onto the path to Ed's orchard. "It was a special privilege to know Ed Edgerton," I said to the TV camera, "and Ed's Camp was a special place. But I'll never come back. It's not the warm and sunny place it used to be. It's a sad and lonely place now, all that was precious about the place I scattered out on the wind this afternoon . . . on one of those warm afternoon breezes I used to enjoy so much."

I've never gone back.

Barbwire deacon of Arizona

Eighty-year old Lyle Linch theorizes, "If you collect a few items of anything in your house, you could rightfully call your house a museum. I just have so much of all these things . . ."

So, at his house in Sunnyslope, which he calls the Echo Museum, every room . . . kitchen . . . bedrooms . . . even the bathroom, boasts collections of lots of stuff. Stuff like: arrowheads, eggbeaters, walking canes, campaign buttons, combs, over 7000 salt and pepper shakers, a collection of thimbles, and several tons of rocks and minerals . . . and a scatology exhibit (if you don't know what that is, look it up).

But, although these collections of things are at least impressive, BARBWIRE is what is king at the Echo Museum. Barbwire is everywhere. The living room walls are covered with hundreds of carefully hand-mounted exhibits of different types of barbwire. His back yard and garage are stacked with buckets of barbwire. In the bathroom, barbwire is embedded in the toilet seat, thankfully far enough into the plastic so nothing sharp sticks out. Of 800 kinds of barbwire in the world, Lyle Linch has samples of 500.

Lyle Linch calls himself, rightfully so, "The Barbwire Deacon of Arizona."

In May of 1983 I met Lyle Linch and he told me of one day many years ago. "So I said I'm gonna get some wire and add it to the top of that fence out there. And a scrounger went by and he had a big coil of wire. And I asked him what he wanted for it and he said 'four bits.' That's fifty cents. And I wasn't dead sure but what I was getting cheated . . . but I gave it to him and I put three wires up on the fence and that very evening I read in *Arizona Highways* where the wire that I got was worth three dollars an eighteen-inch length. And I must of had at least a hundred cuts of wire. I became an ardent barbwire fan . . ."

He chuckles at the memory, beckons me to follow him to the front yard. I follow a tall, slim man who moves with enthusiasm, but an enthusiasm slowed somewhat by all the long years of his life. A straw hat is shoved back on his head; an impressive white goatee falls several inches below his chin . . . bobs up and down when he

talks.

A ramble through Lyle Linch's museum of . . . stuff . . . is well worth the trip.

"This is the President, the white elephant at the top." He shows me a small, porcelain elephant sitting on an upside down cup. He turns the cup over. "And . . . here is what's wrong with the Republican party. You'll notice the handle's on the inside of the cup."

Visitors are given a personal tour of the Echo Museum, a tour which includes an abundance of Linch's personal philosophies and social theories he has intertwined into what he tells you about the thousands of little things he has on neat display. He has many of the answers to life's knotty problems, if only he could get more people to listen. Oddly enough, you often find yourself nodding in agreement . . .

But it is what's in his front yard that might well get him in the *Guinness Book of World Records* where he fervently wants to be. It is a monument to over ten years of patient walking around and around and around. The wearing out of twenty pairs of gloves and the receiving of Lord only knows how many tetanus shots. A rolled up, rusty, untouchable, immovable hulk. It is . . . CLONIA! A seven-foot-high ball of . . . BARBWIRE!

Lyle Linch stands proudly beside this showpiece of the Echo Museum, one hand fondly, but lightly, patting the rusty monster. "The weight is 5275 pounds. That's two and a half tons. The circumference is 22 feet, 4 inches. The miles of wire is fifteen."

No sir. No old ball of string for Lyle Linch. Nothing less than this shrine to years of tying thousands, maybe a million little pieces and scraps and various lengths of old, rusty wire end on end will do. Round and round and round . . .

His motivation? Almost a religious one. "I think I can get this in the book of Guinness." Not the *Guinness Book of Records,* take note, but with reverence . . . awe . . . "THE BOOK OF GUINNESS."

Incidentally, down in the center of all that barbwire there is a silver dollar. If you can reach in and get it, it's yours.

"And I think it's the only dollar in Arizona that's absolutely safe."

*   *   *

A year later now, May 1984. Clonia is fatter by another quarter of a ton and another mile of barbwire. There are plastic ducks perched on top of Clonia, and the tetanus germs have increased by untold billions. And Lyle Linch has cancer . . .

Cancer of the bladder. It will be a fight, he says, then dismisses the subject with a wave of the hand. We won't talk about that anymore.

"Send some of them nice folks from your station down to see my museum. Tell 'em the address. It's 406 East Butler. I'm open 2 to 5 weekdays. There's no charge."

I'm still a little taken aback by this cancer thing. "You'll be here?" I ask.

He pats Clonia affectionately, gently, smiles at me. "I'll be here . . ."

Donnafred

There had been some kind of parade and stuff going on up at Globe. I met Donnafred when I noticed a really strange group of older folks up on the back of a big flat-bed truck hacking and thumping away at washboards and washtubs and anything that would produce some kind of sound. They called themselves the Happy Hayseed Band, made up of senior citizens from the local senior citizen center. They produced as atrocious a sound as you'd ever want to hear.

Well, they had a dancer. Donnafred. Slim, white-haired, attractive, kind of funny black hat. The setting sun tinged orange a little trail of dust she kicked up weaving and swaying to an uncertain beat. Impromptu, to be sure, but graceful and full of undefined meaning, gliding through twists and turns and steps that told some story best known only to Donnafred.

I promptly forgot whatever it was I was filming and did a story about Donnafred and the Happy Hayseed Band. I called her the Dazzling Dancing Damsel of the Desert.

At the time Donnafred gave me a book of poetry she had written. *Pocket Piece, A Collection of Terse Verse.* It contained 100 poems of two to six lines. Terse they were indeed . . . short introspections in verse.

For instance on page 19 . . .

LOST

Can someone tell
the way from Hell?

It seems to lack
a good road back.

On page 33 . . .

LINES TO A LAWN SPRINKLER

Yours is the power
to dispense to the sod
the awaited shower,
to be for an hour
understudy to God.

Page 35 . . .

OVERDONE

Undoubtedly her supine pose
in quite the minimum of clothes
was carefully premeditated.

How innocently does she doze;
I wonder if the lady knows
she's being ultraviolated.

A few months later I went back to visit with Donnafred in her home high on a hill overlooking the east side of Globe. I discovered a fascinating lady. The Dazzling Dancing Damsel of the Desert is not only a poet, she is also a painter and a photographer. She was putting finishing touches on a painting that would be included in her own one-woman show in nearby Claypool.

The show would deal with her impressions of trees and her poetry would be included. Little short poems that described each painting.

"What is the sun but a caster of shadows?"

"In a tangled web of black pine branches winking, fat, old spider moon."

Donnafred's studio is a tangle of impressions of all the years of Donnafred. Paintings scattered about, photographs, ideas scribbled on paper, a busy place.

Her paintings. No particular style, just a whole bunch of styles, she says, all at the same time. I find that over 250 of her paintings are in private collections throughout the U.S. and Canada. And at her most recent showing Donnafred's "Cosmic Color Concert," one of her "abstract" era paintings found its way into my home, too.

Failing eyesight has moved Donnafred into abstract painting, the fine lines of realistic painting are getting harder to see. She should have painted in abstract sooner, the bright splashes of colors form subtle, but not too subtle, impressions, and are a delight. Remembering, please, that I'm not an expert . . . but hopefully I'm not an artistic dunce, either.

Her poetry. Parts of Donnafred's life come pouring out through her poetry.

> You're the one whose kiss
>   I waited for,
> You're the one my line
>   was baited for.
> Tho' the fish in the sea
>   are myriad,
> You're the one,
>   Period!

And . . .

> As a captured eel upon a spit
> doth writhe and squirm,
> So I, impaled upon your rapier wit
> must act the worm.

"I started writing for the **Chicago Tribune**. They had a very famous column, 'A Line O'type or two, let the quips fall where they may'."

Donnafred was born in Iowa and grew up in Minnesota. She married her college chemistry professor, Wilbur Hoff, and they had three children.

> The sound a heart makes when it breaks
> is too small for my ear to hear . . .

If you listen carefully there can be found tiny glimpses into Donnafred's life. Somewhere along the way, there was a devastating, unrequited love.

> You, storm, you have swamped my hold,
> You have broken my single oar.
> You have made me a derelict on my own
> shore.

Unrequited love should teach you something, Donnafred says. Did it, I asked?

> I am habitually caught in summer's drought,
> and fruitless autumn.
> Imprisoned again by your paralyzing winter,
> I dream of spring.
> Her self-perpetuating promise,
> The summer of hope.
> And my tree heavy with fulfillment.
> Earth, I have not learned.

A gentle, sad glance over the top of her glasses. "I guess that answers your question."

She smiles, but for a minute she is somewhere else, somewhere back in memories.

Donnafred. Hard to describe. An older lady pouring out an unending talent up on the top of the hill in a place called Globe, Arizona.

Donnafred. A melancholy lady, so in touch with life and the heart and those special, tender parts of the emotions.

Donnafred. So many of us don't know she's out there. I guess it's always such a surprise to find Donnafreds in places like Globe, Arizona. So many times we don't even look for the Donnafreds in the Globes of the world. Or believe it's even possible for them to be there.

Donnafred. A sensitive, expressive person, not afraid of herself. Moving gently along with the years. With style.

> The past has been pleasant;
> the future looks fine.
> And now, in this present,
> this absolute minute,
> whatever is in it
>   is mine.

Geronimo Altamirano

Geronimo Altamirano never made peace with the white man. One can only assume, then, that any white man who came into his sight . . . was an enemy. Of course, there wasn't much he could do about it back in 1979, when he was reportedly 113 years old, and was living out his long years in a nursing home in Florence.

From what he told Apache historians, though, telling them things that made them believe him, a band of Apache warriors, led by the famous War Chief Geronimo, swooped down and carried him away when he was very young, probably killing his parents.

He was raised as an Apache, and fought against the white man in the late 1800s. We'll never really know the whole story. Geronimo Altamirano only came to the attention of historians in his final years. His memory was fading and he spoke no English and just a little Spanish, and those who spoke Apache and who were interested enough to visit an old, old man, were few and far between. Whatever relatives he had, he outlived.

It means Geronimo Altamirano would have been born in 1866. That would have put him in his late teens when Geronimo was on the warpath through southern Arizona.

In the 1870s and through the late 1880s the Apaches waged an on-again, off-again war with the white man. Names like Cochise and Victorio and Nana and Geronimo sent cold chills through the very souls of settlers and soldiers alike. The Apaches expected, and gave, no quarter and were ruthless and savage warriors.

Geronimo was the last of the Apaches to be on the warpath. He earned himself a place in history as the ultimate holdout, a renegade who fought on past when it was worth fighting, fighting for his freedom and a traditional way of life. Although his war parties seldom numbered over thirty or forty followers, he was so elusive and so well versed in guerilla warfare, that the thousands of troops eventually fielded to capture or kill him . . . never touched him.

Geronimo finally surrendered and was sent to a military reservation in Florida, then to Oklahoma, where he died in 1909, a submissive old man who was never allowed to return to the land of his birth.

There were incidents where bands of raiding Apaches stole young children after massacring the adults. In March of 1883, near Lordsburg, New Mexico Territory, a war party waylaid a buckboard that was carrying a federal judge, H. C. McComas, and his wife and six-year-old son. The Apaches killed both of the adults and took the boy captive.

If the Apaches didn't like the white men, they liked the Mexicans to the south even less, and here again are repeated stories of stealing children and attractive young women. Somewhere along in here, Geronimo Altamirano was taken and, as he grew up, participated in raids on white settlers in Territorial Arizona. Before Geronimo surrendered for the last time, Altamirano apparently left the band and made his own way. Officially, or so he often said, he never made peace with the white man, and spoke of Geronimo as being "muy mal" . . . very bad!

So, as it must be . . . Geronimo Altamirano slipped quietly away from this life. He died in March 1979, at the Pinal County Rest Home in Florence, Arizona.

A sunny, breezy day on the desert west of Florence. There is a cemetery there. A pleasant, tree-shaded lawn with orderly rows of crosses and monuments. Many of the graves have fresh flowers, bright splashes of color on a well-groomed carpet of green. A quiet, dignified place to spend eternity.

The hearse turns into the long drive down the center of the cemetery, a few cars following, rolling slow. That last, sad drive to this nice place where eternity waits out the endless days.

But the small procession keeps rolling. Down at the back of the cemetery the road curves to the right and ends abruptly in a dusty, weed-covered field. HERE is where Geronimo Altamirano will be buried. This windy corner of dust and tumbleweeds and not-so-orderly rows of metal stakes with numbers of them. The Pinal County Pauper's Lot.

Several hundred indistinct graves of those who died without family or identification or means. The numbers on the metal stakes, if you care to spend time, will lead you to the Pinal County Courthouse to some file that will tell you all they know about who's buried under that number. What all they know will be precious little.

The Catholic priest looks distracted, swirls of dust irritate his eyes. He raises his arm over the grave and recites so quickly he almost mumbles, "Eternal rest grant to him, oh Lord. Let perpetual light shine upon him. May he rest in peace. And may his soul, and the souls of all faithfully departed for the mercy of God . . . rest in peace."

Geronimo Altamirano's pallbearers were two men from the funeral home, a local radio personality, and the man who dug the grave. A few friends came to mark the moment, mostly folks from the nursing home, and the import of Geronimo Altamirano's life seemed lost. Nothing was said about his life . . . or about him. He was lowered into the ground . . . in a plywood box.

It all took about five minutes. The man who dug the grave began shovelling dirt into it. His small son, who looked to be about six or seven, shoved dirt in by hand.

I know that when I left, the man climbed on his tractor and bladed the rest of the dirt into the grave. But I will be forever grateful to him for having the sensitivity to take the time to shovel the dirt while I stood there. It seemed, at least, a moment of sensitivity to an old, old man who had come so, so far, and was now beginning his journey to paradise . . . all alone.

* * *

I went back a couple of years later to Geronimo Altamirano's grave and found a simple, nice headstone had been placed there, purchased through the efforts of some of the nurses at the Pinal County Rest Home.

The Gray brothers

The wind at this place comes howling down out of the north with a vengeance. Erasing tracks in the sand, pushing steadily . . . relentlessly . . . forever . . . at man's feeble foothold on the land. Standing here, sand stinging my cheeks, eyes squinted against blowing dust and bright sun, I can't for the life of me figure out why somebody would try to scratch out a living in this place. It would take tough men.

This is the Gachado Well and Line Camp in Organ Pipe Cactus National Monument in southern Arizona. The fence about two hundred feet south is the Mexican border.

"Gachado" is an appropriate name for this lonely place. It comes from "agachado," which in Spanish means to be bent over. And there next to the adobe line cabin is a big old tree, scarred branches bent all the way to the ground in an endless, swaying curtsy . . . paying homage to a hundred years of desert wind. The wind and the desert bent the Gray brothers, too. Made them "gachado." Gachado maybe, but never broken.

The Gray brothers began ranching here in 1919, built a ranch house a mile or so east of Gachado Line Camp. The brothers, Bobby, Henry and Jack, built corrals around the few waterholes there were. Grazing was so poor that cattle ranged far and wide, became wild and mean, and the only way to round them up was to trap them at the waterholes. They built gates that resemble the swinging doors in old west saloons, except these doors only swung one way. When the cow pushed through for a drink of water . . . it couldn't get back out.

They rode this rolling desert of tall cactus cut by rugged peaks for fifty years, through windy cold and blazing heat. It is 1974 now. We are all leaning against a stock tank, a tall windmill creaks occasionally in fitful gusts of hot wind. Water spits from a small pipe into the tank. Bobby and Jack Gray squint over at the Mexican Border.

"Worked a lot of cattle with those Mexican people. Never had no trouble," Bobby reflects. "Fact is, they taught us how to rope Mexican style and handle these damn wild cattle."

Bobby and Jack were handsome men, both in their sixties. Sharp features, deep weather lines around eyes and mouths. The 1970s had been slowly encroaching on their way of life. Their small ranch was eventually surrounded by the National Monument and the Park Service finally rescinded their permits to graze cattle on monument land. The Grays fought that decision in court. There were memories . . .

"There was a lot of dissatisfaction with the government over there." We are still talking about across the fence in Mexico. "They was always rebelling. Always some kind of revolution going on." Bobby slips his hands in his pocket and leans against the stock tank, laughs. "Remember that old plane they sent over, Jack? Had a homemade bomb in it. Open cockpit kind of plane, rattling along. Got a mind it weren't going over eighty mile an hour."

Jack must remember, he chuckles.

"So they made a big circle over there, they circled all over the place. Finally got over there about a mile and threw this ol' bomb out!"

Jack shakes his head. "Didn't wanna throw it out where it'd hurt somebody. It did the job, though, they all pulled out!"

"They took off!" Bobby points. "Thataway! The revolution was over!"

Ah, memories . . .

But the Park Service said, essentially, their ranching days were over. No more grazing.

So the Grays got Senator Carl Hayden to intervene in their behalf. The Secretary of the Interior told the Grays, in this special case, they could graze their cattle as long as they lived. After their deaths no further grazing would be allowed. It was a promise that would be broken.

In 1969 the brothers negotiated a written deal with the Interior Department, agreeing to sell all their improvements and grazing rights. Congress refused to pay, saying the improvements didn't belong to the Grays.

But the cattle continued to graze.

In 1972 the government filed trespass charges against the Grays. And even with support for the Grays by the Arizona Legislature and Arizona's Congressional Delegation in Washington . . . the promise was still broken.

But the legal processes drag on. In December of 1974, on his 65th birthday, and for some reason not fully understood, Jack Gray shot and killed himself.

In September of 1976 the oldest brother, Henry, died of a heart attack. Barely two months later, Bobby, too, died of a heart attack.

The conflict was concluded.

Back to that afternoon in 1974 again, still chewing the rag at the stock tank. Bobby muses, "I think the people still have to eat beef. They claim they have a substitute . . . yeah . . . but I don't think it's too good. I wouldn't wanna eat it myself."

The shadows stretch long across the desert. There's a hitch in Bobby Gray's voice. "You know, they don't want us here. But, by God, we've been here longer'n them. We're Americans. Cowboys. Stockmen. They need us."

* * *

As an epitaph, what Bobby Gray said would surely fade quickly. Eastern feed yards these days raise more prime beef per acre than a western rancher can even imagine. If folks in the National Park Service and various environmental groups had their way, there would be no more western ranches. They don't share, or like, the image of the western cattleman: that romantic, squinty-eyed, leathery, bow-legged hero of Americana. Instead they see him as a raper of the land, a thorn in the side of some hoped for, trackless paradise . . . one of the problems of the west.

So the Gray brothers passed on. All the power of the federal government notwithstanding, they had run their cattle across the desert as long as they lived. It took death to finally arbitrate the conflict in favor of the National Park Service.

"No, I don't regret anything," Bobby Gray told me. "I don't think I'd want to change it much. Liked it pretty well as it was."

The old corral is still around the well at Gachado Line Camp. The water doesn't run anymore, I don't know why. It is ironic that the Park Service now has preserved the old line cabin there, and the original Gray ranch house. Fine examples, they say, of those tough, early ranchers and the lives they led. Nice signs tell a little history about the place and the Grays. Nowhere is there any mention of the conflict.

The use of this desert finally passed fully to the Park Service. But it can never be taken away that it was the tough, iron-willed men of the Old West that tamed places like this. Men like Bobby and Jack and Henry Gray.

And the wind at this place comes howling down out of the north with a vengeance. Erasing tracks in the sand . . . and memories.

Old corral at Gachado Line Camp

What do you give the man who has everything?

A Cow Chip.

YES! Friends and neighbors! A mounted, registered, one of a kind, Arizona Cow Chip! Certain to, ah, surprise that person in your life who has everything. Why do I propose such a gift? A story I did back in 1976.

Even though the sun was barely up, it was hot here a few miles north of Gila Bend. The warm humid of the desert night slowly dissolved into the sticky hot of an August day. It was here where we jumped off into . . . Cow Chip Country. And the hunt was on!

Dave Kline roars past wife Barbara and me and his two small daughters. His Honda XL-100 dirt bike snarls at us as it disappears over a rise in the desert. The pall of dust he leaves behind refuses to settle in the quiet of this God-awful hot morning.

"Uh, breaker-breaker, how do you read this Desert Pete back there in that four-wheeler, come on back?" Channel 19 on a CB radio up under the dash of the jeep we're in. Dave's transmitting to us on a little portable CB radio he carries around his neck. He's half a mile away now and all we can see is his dust, back-lit by an angry, white sun just clearing the horizon.

I'm shooting, tape is rolling, the camera is on Barbara as she picks up the mike, "Uh, read ya' loud and clear, Desert Pete. How do you read me, come on back?" Even through the view-finder I can see she has the mike backwards, the rear of it facing her mouth. She'll probably sound muffled to ol' Desert Pete.

"Uh, you uh, sound just a little muffled, but other'n that, you're loud and clear. Come on ahead, come on back."

"Uh, that's a big ten-four and out."

At the time, Dave Kline was an advertising man in Phoenix, but on weekends his personality shifted from suit and tie to jump suit and hiking boots and an outrageous pair of white sunglasses with red and blue diagonal stripes. Dave Kline and his little portable CB radio and his Honda XL-100 all became part and parcel of the persona "Desert Pete," out leading his stalwart band of cow chip finders, cow chips they will take home and seal in plastic and mount and assign a serial number to . . . and sell.

It is a long, hot day of Desert Pete in the vanguard, and Mrs. Desert Pete . . . and two daughters . . . choking along through his dust, up and down desert washes, over hills. A time-tested method, this scouring of the land for what Dave likes to call a cow chip "gold mine!"

A Desert Pete gold mine is a spot where there is a large concentration of cow chips that have just the right aging and just the right look and . . . well . . . feel.

The hunt is intense, the criteria are exact. Not just any cow chip will do, and the whole family is expert in choosing.

"Well, because it's basically dried out now. And the way we can tell is, when we turn it over, like this, there's no little varmints running out." Dave holds up a massive cow chip, explaining how to read a good one. "If there was still moisture inside somewhere, there would be a lot of little critters of some type bouncing out of there. So, fortunately, there isn't, so it means that now it's nothing more than adobe brick."

I swear to you he almost caresses it. "The best part about it is, it's got nice contour to it, different layers, I think we could consider it a work of art."

Dave Kline's youngest daughter is about four years old and blonde, just as cute as she can be. The paper sack from Safeway is almost as big as she is. She understands what makes a good cow chip, and she has found a perfect specimen. But even at four years old she also understands where the cow chip comes from, and she's not taking any chances. She carries the cow chip daintily between thumb and finger and drops it into the sack, brushes her hands and sticks out her tongue. "Blach!"

Dave smiles at his daughter. "The basic person who's going to buy this is the person with above average income, probably above average education, and the guy who has everything. The guy who's very secure, and has a lot of friends, that, uh, he really can't figure out what to buy them. So, he can buy them a registered cow chip. Because, let's face it . . . how many people do YOU know who have . . . a registered cow chip?"

I have to admit he's got me. "Why isn't this an item for less educated or less income people?" I ask.

"Well, generally, whenever the less educated person looks at this, they don't have an imagination. I don't like to put 'em down or anything, but, they just kinda' look at this and say, 'well, that's just a pile of manure'."

I never was real sure how serious to take Dave Kline, but I guess if people could sell pet rocks, why couldn't he sell cow chips?

We went back to his home later that day and up on a wall in the den were about thirty cow chips, all sealed in plastic, mounted on polished boards. They were, according to what I'd come to understand as the Desert Pete criteria, some of the finest Arizona cow chips available.

"Well, here's what we'd call one of the finest cow chip collections in Arizona." Dave points with pride at the wall. "These are all registered, certified, and a variety of selections."

Dave takes one from the wall. "Each one comes with a registration card which the person fills out and merely drops in the mail, and forever and ever it's filed into permanent history as one of the greatest cow chips . . . and the only one like it . . . as this one right here is, number 39."

He claimed, this Desert Pete AKA Dave Kline, that he sold a lot of these mementos, these bizarre reminders of the Old West. I don't know if he's still in business. I do know I didn't buy one when I had the chance. It would have been too hard to explain.

Trouble with signs and pictures

I drove past this sign several times before I decided to do something about it. It was five feet wide, two feet high . . . large black letters on a yellow background. Black border.

This was in January of 1977. Milepost 301 on Interstate 17, northbound lane, about forty miles south of Flagstaff. For the past month, always the same message screaming out as you pass by . . .

WARNING

Not warning of what . . . just, W A R N I N G ! !

Now, think about it. What's out there? Well, with any imagination at all you can conjure up any danger at all. Ice on the road, maybe? A car-eating monster?

I speculated in a very short story on the air that one frightening possibility was that whatever we were being warned about came along and ate the guy putting up the sign! Ate him before he could get all the sign up.

We can only be left, then, to move on down the road into the unknown, knowing that SOMETHING is out there the Highway Department thought was of enough concern to put up a big sign about.

Be we can be comforted by the fact that, whatever's out there . . . we were warned!

Post-story discovery—the bottom of the sign that should have been attached went on to say . . . "Ice on road next 40 miles." The bottom part had been removed for repairs and someone was lazy about putting it back. Well, you can't be serious all the time.

And talk about not being serious, a few months later in 1977 someone down in Tucson kidnapped Colonel Sanders! Here's what I said in that story . . .

This Kentucky Fried Chicken store is located in southeast Tucson. From almost any place inside one can turn and see a benevolent Colonel Harlan Sanders gazing down on this, another little coop in a vast empire of fried chicken parts. His photograph is, of course, in a spot only slightly less prestigious than the spot where the menu is. What happened here?

"A car pulls up in front," the manager relates, a hurt look in his eyes. "Guy walks in, grabs the picture, walks out just calm as you please."

There are other reporters here. This is a serious story. There is a square, slightly less grungy spot high up the wall where the picture had been. A reporter from another TV station asks, "How long was it before they made the ransom demand?" Somebody snickers.

The manager's eyes dart from reporter to reporter, trying to find which of us is not taking this seriously. "Uh, I believe it took 'em about fifteen minutes."

"Did they call you, or what?"

"Yeah, they called."

"What'd they say when they called?"

"They said, 'We have the picture of the Colonel and we want fifteen buckets of chicken delivered at the handball court at ten o'clock . . . or else!"

The picture is worth maybe twenty-five dollars. Fifteen buckets of chicken are worth almost a hundred dollars. So the kidnappers were reasonable, they lowered their demand to five buckets of chicken.

But there are all sorts of problems here. For instance, how do you know the picture is alive and well? Do you demand to talk to the picture on the phone? If you wait too long will they cut off a piece of the picture and send it to you in the mail to show they're serious? There's just no experience with this sort of thing.

What finally happened is the kidnapper . . . CHICKENED OUT! And made a deal where he would return the picture if promised immunity from prosecution.

So the picture was returned, the kidnapper received no chicken, and employees at this Kentucky Fried Chicken say if anybody else tries to take the Colonel's picture, they're going to have to take the whole wall with it, that's how well the picture will be anchored.

Thank heaven they didn't accede to the kidnapper's demands! Lord only knows what great American Institution they might attack next. Just think how you would feel if they kidnapped Ronald McDonald, or the Jack-in-the-Box Clown.

The Tombstone Epitaph

(...and some other stuff about some other newspapers)

There might be some things in your morning paper you don't like. But that newspaper . . . is a model of taste and truth and wonderfulness compared to the journalism you got back in the formative years of newspapering in the West.

Through the last two-thirds of the nineteenth century, some ten thousand small papers sprouted . . . and mostly withered . . . in the West! Even in the remotest regions, it was a rare gathering of folks and buildings that somebody put a name to that didn't have a newspaper. Denver's *Rocky Mountain News* started in a room above a saloon, and Oregon's *Harney Valley Item* was housed in a former house of ill repute. The Saratoga, Wyoming *Sun* rented out part of their building to a Chinese laundry.

"INDEPENDENCE IN ALL THINGS, NEUTRALITY IN NOTHING" was the masthead of Legh Freeman's *Kearney Herald* started in Fort Kearney, Nebraska Territory, in 1886. That phrase serves in my mind to underscore what western "journalism" was all about for so many colorful and painful years. While Freeman was always one step ahead of somebody wanting to bash in his head for some vitriolic editorial or acutely slanted news story . . . in later years he took on the Mormons in Utah Territory, calling Mormon's plural wives "concubines" and Salt Lake City "a fit place for the Sultan of Turkey" . . . he seems to represent rough and tumble, but not necessarily factual and fair, newspapering of the day.

Of course, newspaper reporters today sort of smile condescendingly during any personal contact with television reporters. We are the upstarts . . . the Johnny-come-latelies to this venerable profession, this telling it like it is stuff, and we have no real grasp of what REAL reporting is all about.

Ah, but let me remind those of the writing press of some of their ancestors. For instance, those editors in the West, who, if they had no real news for their issue, would make something up. Just write some juicy something from straight out of their imagination. And more often than not editorial writing spilled over into what were supposed to be news stories . . . facts laced with personal opinions. It was the way of newspapering . . .

Here in Arizona, in 1880, John Phillip Clum, a former Apache Indian Agent, came to a place called Tombstone and declared, "No tombstone is complete without its epitaph . . .!" And thus started Arizona's oldest continually published, non-daily newspaper, the *Tombstone Epitaph.* And started a chronicle that perhaps best gives us a taste of early-day journalism in our little part of the world.

In 1980, when I did a TV story about the *Tombstone Epitaph,* Harold Love was the editor. He was the kind of guy who would wander happily among the old things in his hundred-year-old building just off Allen Street, this old building where the *Tombstone Epitaph* has always been published, and point out what this was and what that did . . . how it all worked a century ago to put out an average of about two hundred papers a week.

We are sitting in a small room lit by a hanging, bare bulb. All around us are copies of all the *Tombstone Epitaphs* that have ever been printed. Some of the earliest are dry and crinkly, you must handle them with care.

"John Clum, the first editor of the *Epitaph,* came to Tombstone in 1880 from the *Arizona Daily Star* in Tucson." Harold Love traces a finger across the headline of an old *Tombstone Epitaph.* "Silver had been struck here in Tombstone, so he thought this the place to come and make his living."

We shuffle gently through some of the very first *Tombstone Epitaphs.* The comparison is fascinating. These days folks in journalism have to be pretty careful about what they say and have to be able to prove the things they print or air on television. But back in those days . . . well, they could say about anything they wanted.

"It wasn't uncommon for John Clum and the editors of the other, more transitory papers in town to get into some really nasty word duels in their columns," relates Love. "Seems like none of them ever liked each other, and it really got personal! In print they'd call each other "despicable," "swine," "sotted." They'd stab at each other with flowery references dealing with a person's ability to hold liquor, write eloquent passages about his mental capabilities, and freely question the other's heritage. All in print. Sometimes in

The Tombstone Epitaph

NO.   TOMBSTONE, COCHISE COUNTY, ARIZONA, THURSDAY MORNING OCTOBER 27, 1881.

YESTERDAY'S TRAGEDY

Three Men Hurled Into Eternity in the Duration of a Moment.—

Stormy as were the early days of Tombstone, nothing ever occurred equal to the event of yesterday. Since the retirement of Ben Sippy as marshal and the appointment of V. W. Earp to fill the vacancy, the town has been noted for its quietness and good order. The frequent row that formerly much dreaded now bore when they came to town were upon their good behavior, and so unseemly brawls were indulged in, and it was hoped by our citizens that no more such deeds would occur as led to the killing of Marshal White, one year ago. It seems that this quiet state of affairs was but the calm that precedes the storm that burst in all its fury yesterday, with the difference in results, that the lightning's bolt struck in a different quarter than the one last fall one year ago. This time it struck with its full and awful force upon three men, heretofore, have made the good name of this country a byword and a reproach, instead of upon some officer in the discharge of his duty or a peaceable and unoffending citizen. . . .

Some time Tuesday The Clanton came into town, and during the evening had some little talk with Doc Holliday and Marshal Earp, but nothing that caused either to suspect, further than their general knowledge of the man and the threats that had previously been conveyed to the Marshal that the gang intended to clean out the Earps, that he was thirsting for blood at this time, with one exception, and that was that Clanton had told the Marshal, in answer to a question, that the McLowrys were in Sonora. Shortly after this occurred some one came to the Marshal and told him the McLowrys had been seen a short time before, just before. Marshal Earp, not knowing what might happen and feeling his responsibility for the preservation of the peace and order of the city, called on duty all night and aided the police force his brother Morgan and Holliday. The night passed without any disturbance whatever, and at sunrise he went home and retired to rest and sleep.

A short time afterward one of his brothers came to his house and told him that Clanton was hunting him, with threats of shooting him on sight. He disrobed the report and did not get out of bed. It was not long before another of his brothers came down and told him the same thing, whereupon he got up, dressed and proceeded down town, where he met Morgan on the street.

They walked up Allen street to Fifth, crossed over to Fremont and down to Fourth, where, upon turning up Fourth toward Allen, they came upon Clanton, with a Winchester rifle in his hand on a revolver on his hip. The Marshal walked up to him, grabbed the rifle and hit him a blow at the same time on the head, stunning him so that he was able to disarm him without further trouble. He marched Clanton off to the police court, where he entered complaint against him for carrying deadly weapons, and the court fined Clanton $25 and costs, making $27.50 altogether. This occurrence must have been about 1 o'clock in the afternoon.

THE AFTER-OCCURRENCE.

Close upon the heels of this came the finale, which is best told in the words of R. F. Coleman, who was an eye-witness from the beginning to the end. Mr. Coleman says: I was in the O. K. Corral at 2:30 p. m., when I saw the two Clanton's (Ike and Bill), and the two McLowry boys (Frank and Tom), in earnest conversation across the street, in Dunbar's corral. I went up the street and notified Sheriff Behan, and told him it was my opinion they meant trouble, and that it was his duty, as Sheriff, to go and disarm them; I told him they had gone to the West End Corral. I then went and saw Marshal Virgil Earp, and notified him to the same effect. I then met Billy Allen, and we walked through the O. K. Corral, about fifty yards behind the Sheriff. On reaching Fremont street I saw Virgil Earp, Wyatt Earp, Morgan Earp and Doc Holliday, in the center of the street, all armed. I had reached Behan's meat market; John-by Behan had just left the two boys, after having a conversation with them. I went along to Fly's photograph gallery, when . . .

CORONERS INQUEST

JOSEPH ISAAC CLANTON

. . . rowers, said; My name is Joseph I. Clanton, commonly known by the sobriquet "Ike" . . . (Clanton county; am brother to William Clanton who was killed; saw the whole affair. Night before the shooting went into the Occidental (keno house) to bank. While there Doc Holliday came in and commenced abusing me; had his hand on his gun all the time and called me a d—d son of a b—; told me that I was a cowboy and a thief and that I could whip me. I told him that I was not heeled. Just at that point Morg Earp came up with his gun on and said, "You d—d son of a b—, if you are so anxious to make a fight, I will give you one." I told them all that I did not want to fight, as I was not heeled. Looking around I saw Ike Earp standing at the bar with his hand on his gun. Doc Holliday kept abusing me until I went out. Virg Earp, Wyatt Earp and Morgan Earp were there; they told me I pushed a fight to have myself heeled. All bad their hands on their guns while they were talking. Holliday said, "I've not a d—d son of a bitch yourself." I went off and felt myself. Came back soon and played poker with Virg Earp, Tom McLowry and others. Virg had his gun on top of the time. At daylight we quit, About 8 o'clock in the morning I went and got my Winchester, depending to meet Doc Holliday on the street, but never saw him until Virg and Morg Earp slipped up behind me and knocked me down with a six-shooter. Soon after I came up I saw the two McLowry boys. I told them about being arrested and taken out of town. We went to the West End corral every day soon. There we met Sheriff Behan. He said he would have to arrest us and take us into custody. I told him that we were going, out of town right away. He then told Billy to come up to him where he sat and gave up his arms. Billy told him he was just leaving town, but if the sheriff would disarm the Earps he would give up his arms. The sheriff said he would have to arrest us and take our guns. They went right by. I advanced two or three steps from the crowd and met Wyatt Earp at the corner of the building. He stuck his six-shooter in and said, "Throw up your hands." The Marshal also said to the other boys, "Threw up your hands." They said "You son of a b—, you have come to make a fight. At the same instant Doc Holliday and Morg Earp shot; Morg shot Bill Clanton, and I don't know which of the boys Holliday shot; saw Virg Earp shooting at the same time. I pushed Wyatt Earp around the corner of the house and jumped into the gallery; as I jumped I saw Doc Holliday run through the photograph gallery and got away. When ordered to hold up our hands, we all held them up, except Tom, who held open his coat to show that he was unarmed. There was nothing between the Earps and ourselves but ready to make their own move; they were yet ready for business; I had no arms whatever about me; I ran at Wyatt Earp and the others began to shoot. At the request of Major Frink, Behan saw the Earps coming but he did; he told us to stay there. After the sheriff left I would not stay; only the sheriff told me to. Behan was with the boys long enough to say what I have before stated.

JOHN H. BEHAN

. . . was sworn, and testified as follows: About 2:30 I was in the barber's shop, and heard of trouble between the Clantons and Earp. I went over to Hafford's corner. I asked Virgil Earp, the marshal, what was the excitement. He said there was a lot of s—s looking for a fight. He mentioned no names. I said to Earp, "I've had better disarm the crowd." He said he would not, but would give them a chance to make a fight. I said, "It is your duty as a peace officer to disarm the parties." I meant any parties connected with the cow boys who had arms. Morgan Earp and Holliday were the ones I was talking to at the intersection of Allen and Fourth. Virgil Earp had a shotgun. I saw no arms on the others. I then went down Fourth street to the corner of Fremont and crossed to the opposite side of Fourth street and saw Frank McLowry holding a horse and in conversation with somebody. I told McLowry I would have to disarm him; that there was likely to be some trouble in town and I proposed to disarm everybody that had an arm. He said he would not give up his arm; that he didn't like to lose any trouble. I instated, About that time I saw the Clanton and Tom McLowry were standing. I said to Frank, "Come with me." We went to where Ike Clanton and Tom McLowry were standing. I said to them, "Boys, you must give up your arms." Billy Clanton and William Claiborne, alias Billy the Kid, were there. Frank McLowry demurred. Ike Clanton told me he was unarmed. I put my arm around his waist and found he was not armed. Tom McLowry pulled his coat open and showed me he was not armed. I saw five standing there and asked how many there were of their party. They said four. Claiborne said he was not one of them; that he was there wanting them to leave town. I said, "Boys, you must go up to the sheriff's office, by aside your arms, and stay till I get back." I told them I was going to disarm the party. At that time I saw Earps and Holliday coming down the south side of Fremont street. They came by the post-office and Bauer's shop. I mean Morg Earp and the t— . . .

Fremont Street.

[illustration of street scene]

. . . fired by the Earp party. I thought the next three shots came from the same side, but was not certain; it is only my impression. After the words "throw up your hands" immediately the nickel-plated pistol went off. I saw Frank McLowry with one hand to his belly and with his right hand shooting toward Morgan Earp. As he started across the street, I heard a couple of shots from a direction in which Frank McLowry was. I looked and saw him running and a pistol went off and he fell over on his head; I heard Morg Earp say, "I've got him." There may have been a couple of shots aftenward, but that was the end of the fight. I did not see the effect of the two first shots that were fired; the only portion I saw was Frank McLowry and Morgan Earp. I saw an effect from the next three shots. The first shot that I thought was Wyatt Earp's McLowry. I saw him staggering and bewildered shortly after the first few shots. I never saw any arms in the hands of any-body of the McLowry party except Frank McLowry and Billy Clanton. I saw Frank McLowry on the side with a six-shooter in the line of the fire of the two; I think that eight or ten shots had been fired be fore I saw arms in the hands of any of the McLowry or Clanton party. Frank McLowry was the first man I whose hands I saw a pistol. After the first few shots, Ike Clanton broke and ran. I saw him at the back building.

The Continuation of Sheriff Behan's

DIRECT EXAMINATION.

Ike Clanton broke and ran I did not know where he went. I found him afterward in Kemmell's building on Tough Nut street. I saw a shotgun with Holliday before the fight commenced, as they were coming down the street. He had it under his coat. I did not see the gun go off, and if I heard the report I did not distinguish it from a pistol. . . After we examined Billy Clanton, before he died, as he was lying in the street. . After he was taken in the house all I heard him say was to go away and let him die. . I saw him when he was lying on the sidewalk, and saw him when Morgan Earp shot him. A number were with him, one Billy Clanton was carried in. Dr. Gibson said it was no use to give him anything. I left before Billy Clanton died. He was gasping when I left. Tom McLowry's body was in the same room.

CROSS EXAMINATION.

Was in town the entire day of the twenty-sixth. I knew the night before that there had been a row between Holliday and Clanton. The first intimation I had of the anticipated difficulty between the Earp party and the Clanton party I received in the barber's shop. I had heard the night before of a difficulty between Ike Clanton and Doc Holliday. Heard of it about 2:30 or 3 o'clock. Had not heard of any difficulty between Virgil Earp and Ike Clanton. First heard, while in the barber shop, of a difficulty between Wyatt Earp and Tom McLowry that had taken place in the neighborhood of Wallace's office. I was in Hafford's saloon ten or fifteen minutes before the fight. I procured Allen street to acompany with one Charles A. Shibell. I don't remember whether I saw Virgil Earp there or not. I may have said to Virgil Earp there, "We are going to make a drink; will you join us?" I don't remember that Virgil Earp join us in a drink. I don't remember of saying when we, while we were there, Captain Murray came in and called Virgil Earp away on the lower end of the counter.

Question: Do you remember that when Virgil Earp came back from Murray to where you were standing, you said to him, "What does that son of a b—h of a strange want?" Answer: I don't remember it, and I am satisfied that no such words passed my lips, as Captain Murray and myself were on friendly terms.

Q. Do you remember that you then asked Virgil Earp what he was going to do? A. "No, I don't recollect."

Q. Do you remember Virgil Earp replying, "I am going to disarm them?" A. No.

Q. Do recollect replying to that remark: "Don't undertake to do that, or they will kill you," referring to the Clanton crowd, "they were just down in my corral, having a gun talk against you, and threatening your life?" A. "No such conversation ever happened, and they made no such reply, for I had not been down in my corral."

Q. Do you recollect further saying, "I will go down where they are; they won't hurt me, and I will get them to lay off their arms?" A. This conversation did not take place at that time.

Q. Did you subsequent to the fight, somewhere in the city of Tombstone, and upon the day of the fight, and in speaking of the fight between the Earp crowd and the Clanton crowd, say to Charles Shibell, that it was a dead, square fight, and that you could not tell which shot fired first? A. No.

Q. Did you not make that remark or one of like import to Wyatt Earp after the fight, on the corner of Fremont and Third streets, and upon the day of the fight? A. No, sir.

Q. Did you see anybody take a pistol from the hand of Billy Clanton? A. I did not; I was engaged with Billy Claiborne.

Q. After the fight was over, how soon did you leave the battle ground, and where did you go? A. Probably four or five minutes. I went up Fremont street, to Hafford's corner, where I saw a lot of armed men; and Wyatt Earp near the corner of Fremont and Fourth streets. I had a . . .

THE B—

[advertising column]

Clot

Where you . . .
Consumers . . .
saving and the like . . .
quickest and . . .

205 | OUR

Shee
Better wo—
and pump wo—
and cheapest
First-Class T—

PIONEER

212

DEALER IN
CHINE
The Only

CLAPP

INSURA
508

COMB—
of C—

$75,

ACCO—

Fa—

Ari—

the editorial column, sometimes elsewhere in the newspaper. A lot of times they'd get into fistfights when they met each other on the street."

But for all that, the **Tombstone Epitaph** also told it like it was. There is the copy of the paper Thursday morning, October 27, 1881 . . .

"THREE MEN HURLED INTO ETERNITY IN THE DURATION OF A MOMENT!" The gunfight at the OK Corral! Hurled into eternity in the duration of a moment! Oh boy, how much better could you tell it! Sometimes I think we in modern journalism could take lessons from the boys back then. The **Epitaph** told the story in page after page, and gave us the best account we have of how the Clantons and McLawrys and Earps and Doc Holliday blazed away at each other in a dusty lot near the OK Corral in the Old West.

On that day in 1980 when I did the television story, the **Tombstone Epitaph** . . . a hundred years old . . . was called "The Paper Too Tough To Die," paraphrasing, of course, what they call Tombstone, "The Town Too Tough To Die." But, it's not what it used to be. Oh, they still publish once or twice a month, a sort of historical journal and a few news stories, and still do things the old way with the old press . . . and the romance of it all kinda hangs heavy in the air . . . a smell of ink and heat, if you will. Imagined smells of violence and romance in the Old West.

But there is a musty smell, too. Especially in this room among these hundred-year-old copies of the **Tombstone Epitaph**. A musty old newspaper and musty old words about a different time.

So, if there are things in your morning paper you don't like, think of how it used to be. The editor of your newspaper probably won't question your personal heritage. At least not in these pages.

Dancing to a different beat

"I'm not a sheepherder. I'm a city boy."

Fifteen-year-old Karl Carlos Kai is a full-blood Navajo, speaks Navajo, looks like a Navajo, but he will never BE a Navajo. He will never be a sheepherder. In this instance the long ties to land and tradition are broken. Karl Kai, Navajo, is a Break-Dancer. His friends know him by his break-dancing nickname, K.C.K.

"I like to get around," says K.C.K. "Get dressed up slick and go to town, go out and strut and rap and do a little dancin'."

When K.C.K. gets dressed up slick he's wearing parachute pants, Nike jacket with hood (100 percent all-American nylon), specially decorated tennis shoes with wide, untied laces, a leather strap with spikes on the wrist . . . maybe one around the neck . . . a rising sun bandanna around the head, all topped with a crazy black hat. He hits the streets with his girlfriend, "Sweet C," on his arm.

Karl Kai used to go to the reservation school at Dilcon, on the Navajo Reservation just north of Winslow. He left and moved to Winslow with his parents and when he came back to visit his friends, he brought a whole new idea with him.

Dilcon School is run by the Bureau of Indian Affairs and has about 600 Navajo students from this southern part of the vast reservation. For many Navajos, a place like Dilcon School is a social hub of activities, a gathering place. It's rare a grade B movie ever gets to most parts of the reservation, and if it does, it will probably be shown in a school auditorium.

For centuries, musical entertainment for Navajos has been the sound of drums and age-old chants and songs handed down across time. But, with battery-powered radios and televisions in remote hogans, rock and roll and country and western music and the ideas and fads they bring has crept into the stoic, reserved nature of Navajos. Especially the young Navajos, who see a whole new, bright world out there that seems to offer an attractive alternative to a lifetime of far-away-from-anyplace, awful drudgery . . . a lifetime of living on a lonely land.

So, young Navajos break away from the land. And nowhere is it more evident than at the Dilcon School where K.C.K. brought

break-dancing to some of the students there.

It's a hard image to conjure up, this idea of a Navajo break-dancer. But, after a time in the big city of Winslow, Karl Kai got slicked up and strutted back to see his friends at Dilcon School. And for about 15 or 20 of them, dancing was never the same.

Break-dancing is danced to a kind of music I don't understand. Of course you have to realize a statement like that is made by each generation to the following one. My folks said it to me, their folks said it to them, and so on. I used to think I was cool when I was a teenager and snaked across the gym floor, undulating to the jungle beat of Elvis Presley and Little Richard. I was hep. Not hip, hep!

I may not understand the music, but the steps fascinate me, dazzle me. The robot-like movements, leaps, falls, whirls, they spend as much time writhing on the floor as they do dancing on it with their feet. Somewhere in their bodies break-dancers have a high rpm motor that engages automatically at a certain body-thumping beat at some very high decibel level and powers them through their moves. A motor most of us don't have.

"Navajo kids are normally inhibited," says Don Decker, a counselor at Dilcon School. "I view this break-dancing as healthy. . . it lets them break out and show their individuality. Other schools on the reservation are doing it to some extent. The kids even have break-dancing contests between the schools." Decker smiles proudly at the dancers. "We usually win."

Karl Carlos Kai, K.C.K., is the sort of Guru of break-dancers here, the idolized founding father of THE dance, the man with THE moves. When K.C.K. dances, everybody steps back, gives him room. K.C.K.'s motor is wound tighter, produces more rpms, is more finely tuned. He walks hip, talks hip, dances ultra-hip, K.C.K. IS hip.

K.C.K. goes to Winslow Junior High and I asked him, "How did you pick up these moves? Did you copy them from what you saw on television?"

"Man, I might have got the idea from there, but I got my OWN moves. I got K.C.K. moves. That's what it's all about, man."

"They pattern themselves to the overwhelming, predominant customs. In this case it's white man's customs," says Decker.

"Isn't there a danger, then, that a culture will be diluted and eventually disappear?" I asked. "Doesn't the language go, then identity?"

"It's not the death of a culture. I think many of these kids will return to a sense of their birthplace, will learn to live in a bi-cultural atmosphere. It's something the white man would be better off with if he could learn to live with cultures other than his own."

K.C.K. is telling me about his grandparents. "My grandparents, well, I showed them my dance once." K.C.K. smiles at the memory. "They thought I had gone crazy. They are old traditional Navajos. They wanted to know if I was on drugs.

"I tried to tell them what I do, why I dress this way, about going out on the streets with my friends to strut, to rap. They didn't understand. We don't talk about it anymore."

K.C.K. teaches a class in break-dancing in Winslow to a dozen kids ranging in age from four to thirteen years old. He wants to be a professional dancer. He doesn't particularly want to go back to the reservation.

"It's boring, the Navajo way . . ."

The man who tied a knot in the Devil's tail

Although the sun was shining down from a cloudless, dazzling blue sky, it shone on a foot of snow and an afternoon of windless, but biting cold. It made the fireplace in the old house on the corner of Gurley and North Mt. Vernon streets in Prescott a crackling circle of warmth and refuge . . . a good place to sit and talk and tell stories and stare into the flames . . . safe from the lengthening shadows and deepening cold of this January afternoon in 1979.

I was visiting eighty-six-year-old Gail Gardner, poet, cowboy, historian, postmaster, fine gentleman. He lived in this house his father built back before the turn of the century, the house he was born in. His father had come to Prescott lured by the promise that it was a gambler's paradise.

Slanted sunlight streams in the west-facing windows and is the only light in the huge living room. Gail Gardner, a slight man who walks with the burden of his years, sits on a long couch in front of the fireplace. Time has dimmed his vision and he wears thick glasses, the lens over the left eye is dark, and he seems to watch you only vaguely. It is a quiet room, heavy with memories of the comings and goings of almost a hundred years.

For twenty years Gail Gardner was Prescott's postmaster, but some of his fondest memories are of the days he was a cowboy.

"I had a little greasy-sack cow outfit in Skull Valley from about 1916 on . . . for two or three years. But I kept that little old ranch and didn't sell it until 1960." Gail Gardner scratches his ear. Memories.

"Them was the best years, I tell ya. Yessir . . . wide open spaces and clean air and ridin' the high country on your own . . ." Memories.

He remembers the violence of Prescott in the early days, at least before one particular U.S. Marshal came to town. "One time they, uh, these cowboys . . . they did come in with the idea of shooting up the town. Well, they had a United States Marshal here . . . I believe Father said his name was Jimmy Dodson . . . and when these cowboys came in and shot up the town, why this United States Marshal just followed up and killed two or three of 'em and that ended shootin' up Prescott!" He laughs.

Over the fireplace in Gardner's home is a painting by the late George Phippen. It is a graphic and exciting portrayal of two cowboys, obviously in their cups, lassoing the Devil. The Devil in the painting is an evil-looking, angry fellow with horns and forked tongue and cloven hooves and a pointy tail. He's madder'n hell at one lasso over his horns and another around his hooves.

The painting was prompted by a poem that Gail Gardner wrote. And the poem was prompted by something a cowboy friend of his said late one night, when they found themselves alongside a creek, splashing water on their faces, trying to wash away the effects of a hard night's drinking along Prescott's Whiskey Row.

Sandy Bob turned to Gail Gardner and remarked, "I believe the Devil hisself is gonna get us for drinkin' like this."

Years later, Gardner wrote a poem called "Tying a Knot in the Devil's Tail." It imagines what might have happened if ol' Sandy Bob and Gardner...whose nickname in those days was Buster Jig...had actually met the Devil that one drunken night.

> "He says, hey you ornery cowboy skunks, you'd better hunt your holes, 'cause I've come up from Hell's rimrock, to gather in your souls.
> "Says Sandy Bob, ol' Devil be-damned! We boys is kinda' tight, but ya ain't gonna gather no cowboy's souls without ya has some kinda fight.
> "So Sandy Bob punched a hole in his rope and he swang her straight and true. He lapped it onto the Devil's horn and he takin' his dallies, too.
> "Now Buster Jig was a reata man, with his gut-line coiled up neat. So he shakin' her out and built him a loop, and he lass'd the Devil's hind feet.
> "Oh, they stretched him out and tailed him down, an' while the irons was a'gettin' hot, they cropped an' forked his ears...and they branded him up a lot.
> "They pruned him up with a de-hornin' saw an' knotted his tail for a joke. .. and then rid off and left him there, necked to a blackjack oak."

The winter afternoon fades, another log goes on the fire, and more and more now we find ourselves in the midst of long silences...chins propped in our hands, eyes searching the fire for...well...nothing really, just the easy, almost sleepy pleasantness of this warm room. Talk turns to warmer, sunnier days already gone by. And to things you might hear way up high in the "Siry

Petes" (Sierra Prietas) west of Prescott. Things you might hear on the wind . . .

> "If you're ever up high in the 'Siry Petes', and ya hear one helluva wail . . . you'll know it's that Devil a bellerin' around . . . about them knots in his tail."

Be careful up there . . . I can tell you, that Devil is UPSET!

Old Route 66 over Sitgreaves

August 1979

At first they came up this long valley west of Kingman and over this mountain pass in their wagon trains. And then later they came up the road in their model A's and model T's, up this road that was once called "The Mainstream of America."

A lot of dreams came over this pass . . . heading west, heading for California, leaving behind forever the broken dreams of depression years and dust bowls and misery back somewhere east of here. They came here, a lot of people liked to say, mostly from Oklahoma and Arkansas, and they called them the Okies and the Arkies. But really they came from everywhere . . . the misery of those days just seemed to have no hometown.

This is Sitgreaves Pass. This is a still place in time, a high place of ghosts and memories, a place where a road carried the folks along their way to a new hope. The road is still here, but the dreams are not, and it only carries an occasional traveler up its twisting, narrow and steep and sometimes scary grade. Travelers who mostly promise themselves never to come this way again because of all the potholes and vague memories of yellow lines that divide a road so narrow it's a nerve-shattering test of perception to meet and pass another car coming the other way. But this snake of crumbling blacktop up over the Black Mountains was once THE way to go from east to west . . . Route 66.

In its day it was a marvel of engineering and construction, but in 1951 it was abandoned. Today one can only imagine the transcontinental traffic, both wagon trains and motorized vehicles . . . only imagine faint echoes of the strain this part of Route 66 put on travelers.

Way back, of course, it wasn't called Route 66, it was called the Immigrant Trail. Wagon trains crossed the Black Mountains along here, the army used this pass to supply old Fort Mohave down on the Colorado River.

At the turn of the century one of Arizona's last gold boomtowns flourished on the western slopes of this mountain range, Oatman,

Old Route 66 over Sitgreaves

and a major highway, Highway 66, was built to it.

Over on the east side of the pass, just as the road gets started into the series of steep turns and switchbacks that made it so treacherous, there is a place called Ed's Camp. The Ed of Ed's Camp was Ed Edgerton. He's dead now, but he had been there for over fifty years. For many years Ed's Camp was a gas station and restaurant. Tall trees grew, there was an orchard, it was a green, cool place in a little canyon.

Years ago Ed Edgerton told me forty buses a day stopped there and model A's and T's would line up waiting for the cool of the evening before attempting what was called one of the most feared mountain crossings in the entire length of U.S. 66.

If you stop at Ed's Camp today there will almost always be a soft wind through the leaves of the tall trees, whispering stories of the people who stopped there. There were so many who waited at this oasis, this last friendly outpost, before struggling on up a road Henry Ford had never designed his car for, and there were many who just never made it to the top of the Pass. They "busted."

Up at the top of the pass several of us are standing around, marveling at the view. With us is Roman Malach. He is an historian, and an authority on the history of this part of the state. He likes to talk about the travelers who came this way . . .

"Well, I related to you a description a lady wrote who traveled this way in a Model T. She and many other writers would speak about this as the most dangerous piece of road in the United States back then.

"I think the hardship behind those early travelers is impossible for us to understand . . . to believe . . . or whatever you want to say. The heat and the physical work and danger and the daily fear you weren't going to get to someplace where there was only a promise of better things.

"We soft Americans . . . look, there is a car going on his way without even paying any attention to what on earth was happening here fifty or sixty or seventy years ago."

Roman Malach points down the mountain to a car that is coming up the old highway. The car will accomplish without effort . . . and in just a few minutes . . . a task that sometimes not too long ago was sometimes the final straw, a task that broke strong men.

Actually, it doesn't take more than five minutes today to

negotiate the twisty turns from the valley floor to the top of the pass. These are not TALL mountains, these Black Mountains, they are just steep and craggy and sunbaked. In some ways you can imagine this is the way the surface of the moon must look. Hot winds blow up from the Colorado River Valley to the west, scorching the rocks, super-heating the air. Man would never have stayed here if there wasn't gold hidden away in the rocks.

Not too long ago, though, a journey up this pass, whether wagon train or model T, was something you remembered all your life. It was one of the obstacles on the way west.

The car hums by us leaving a short blast of wind and a swirl of dust, disappears down the other side of the pass, moving west. Moving west over an old, abandoned road that carried dreams. Some dreams that never made it. A symbol of those shattered dreams lies off the road about a quarter mile down the west side of the pass . . . the hulk of an old model T . . . lying a-rusting in the long shadows of afternoon, no hint of what happened to its long ago owner. Where did he go from here . . . whatever happened to him?

This is Old Route 66 over Sitgreaves Pass, a road that today snakes its way through a lot of memories. Forgotten memories . . . not very important anymore.

The Sinagua at Walnut Canyon

I have this picture in my mind and I wonder if it's possible this could have happened. Running-Man is standing on the ledge in front of his home built under the cliff overhang about 200 feet below the rim of the canyon. The evening is cool, sky is clear, a quiet night is coming on. In the distance, across the canyon, Running-Man sees his good friend and hunting buddy, Rising-Moon. Cupping his hands Running-Man yells, "HEY, RISING-MOON! WHATCHA' DOIN'? BRING THE LITTLE LADY OVER AND LET'S BARBECUE SOME VENISON!"

I'm not trying to be flippant and this may be a little too simplistic, but did Sinagua Indians do that sort of thing? Did the Hohokam, or Anasazi? Or was it up at dawn, work like a dog all day, tear off a few bites of jerky at night and hit the sack? I do know it aggravates archeologists when I ask them to give me some idea of these people's personalities. I know they had dances and religious things and games and they had languages and could communicate ideas. But did they ever sit around out on the "patio" and watch the sun go down and maybe have a sociable drink and verbalize abstract thoughts?

It aggravates me and it aggravates archeologists because we don't really have enough information to answer such a question. The Sinagua and Anasazi and Hohokam left a lot behind, but they took the soul of their existence with them. They took their private thoughts and their abstract ideas and their loves and hates with them. We can only guess.

I try to imagine these sort of things when I go to a place like Walnut Canyon. Walnut Canyon is about 10 miles east of Flagstaff and not one of the major archeological sites in the west. It is impressive, though, as an example of transition of the Sinagua from simple pithouse dweller to a culture of more sophisticated architecture and arts and crafts and religion.

Unfortunately, since Walnut Canyon is so close to a major cross-country thoroughfare, that has seen the passage of countless people for more than a century and a half, that by the time archeologists arrived, the ruins had been stripped by vandals and pothunters. So, most of what is known about the people who lived here comes from excavations at other, similar sites of the same period.

The trail visitors take to see the ruins is about three-quarters of a mile long and the first, and last, part is a steep, 200 foot climb. You climb down stairs cemented into the canyon side, there's an easy walk around a sort of island jutting up out of the canyon floor, then loop back and return UP the same stairs. The trail meanders along the base of a cliff past ancient dwellings that have remained here in various states of deterioration for seven or eight centuries.

The Walnut Canyon Sinagua built their small masonry structures in cliff overhangs in this deep canyon that had a year-round stream flowing in the bottom. They were farmers and hunters. Their structures were a far cry from the great Anasazi cliff dwellings, but they were safe and secure and efficient and in tune with the

environment.

Walnut Canyon in the 12th century must have hummed with life. As many as 500 people at any one time lived here between the early 1100s and well into the 13th century. Probably, as with the Anasazi, drought and overuse of the land sent the Sinagua away. They moved into the Verde Valley and stayed there until the 1400s. Where they went after that can't be said with certainty.

Walnut Canyon is a good place to come to and wonder about things like whether or not the Sinaguas got together in the evening and chatted abstract things. Not a lot of people come here and it's easy to sit for awhile in one of the ancient structures and gaze off across the canyon and listen to the wind for a hint, a whisper, of the emotions the Sinagua felt when they sat in the same place.

"We must leave this place, Rising-Moon. The water comes less and less each season. I think this season it will not run the whole time, and the land won't get as green as it used to. We must follow the water." Running-Man stares off into a pink, fading sky. A star twinkles on the horizon. "I am sad, I love this place. My children were born here, my parents, their parents."

Rising-Moon wraps his arm around Man's shoulders. "Things will be better, Running-Man. We've always managed. We always will."

Darkness flowed into the canyon, the night was quiet. It was all a long time ago. The Sinagua departed into the dust of the centuries . . .

The light of the longest day

It is a place to fire the imagination. It is a place that was once a vast swamp roamed by creatures straight out of a nasty dream. A place where pre-historic monsters the size of a Greyhound bus tromped across the land, and crocodile-like beasts weighing a ton or more came slithering up out of the water.

Thank heaven that was millions of years ago because this place is just a few miles east of Holbrook, Arizona, and I wouldn't sleep at all if I knew creatures like that were loose in the night, just over a few hills from me.

It is a place called Petrified Forest National Park. And the monsters and the swamps went away as the millenniums piled up and turned into millions and then hundreds of millions of years. It became a desert. And maybe about a thousand years ago, a mere blink of the eye of time, an Indian civilization came here. Then they, too, went away.

And just a few years ago, a fellow by the name of Dr. Robert Preston, an astronomer at Jet Propulsion Laboratory, came to Petrified Forest and stood and gazed at a slab of boulder called Newspaper Rock, so-called because of all the petroglyphs carved on it by the Anasazi Indians. Carvings that folks today don't really have much idea what they all mean.

Well, Dr. Preston was just being a tourist, on vacation, and he stared and stared at one particular petroglyph. It was a large circle that spiraled in on itself, gradually becoming smaller and smaller until it stopped at a point in the center. It almost looked like someone's idea of a crude bulls-eye. It reminded Dr. Preston of an astronomy symbol...

"He thought they were related to the sun and its movement, and he started doing some initial investigations when he was here." Roger Rector was the superintendent of the park when I was there doing the story. "And he very much determined that it was solar-related. He asked for permission to do further studies during solstice and equinox periods throughout one full year.

"They found 19 sites throughout the state of Arizona, 14 of them within Petrified Forest, that were solar related."

One of those sites that marked the summer solstice is at the Puerco Indian ruin in the park. On June 21st, early in the morning, a shaft of sunlight begins a creeping journey across a rock. The rock lies in the midst of a jumble of boulders near the ruin, and down the side of the rock a circle is carved. A petroglyph. What looks like a capital J that fell over on its right side is inside the circle.

There are tourists standing nearby, cameras at the ready, a ranger explaining what's happening. The shaft of light spills over the edge of the rock now, begins a slow descent toward the petroglyph.

Roger Rector and I sit on the flat top of a huge boulder peering down at the shaft of sunlight inching its way down the rock. "Some of the things that were related to the solar system would have had a definite interaction with the life that they were living each day," Roger said. "It was important to them that they would have something that would determine some of these things that were so important to their livelihood."

The shaft of sunlight is long and narrow, and advances on the circular petroglyph. A spooky connection to dusty past now. What old Anasazi man sat where I now sit and watched the same thing?

Finally, the sunlight pierces the petroglyph, rests perfectly in the cradle formed by the fallen capital J, and by a trick of rock and shadow, goes no farther. It is the longest day of the year. Every June 21st it happens. Not on the 20th or the 22nd.

There is an undeniable fascination here. An ancient man somehow, somehow understood the movement of the planet in relation to the sun, and carved a precise notice of the longest day of the year.

On the Hopi Mesas, 70 miles to the northwest, the Home Dances begin. Hundreds of years ago, this might have been the way the Anasazis knew it was time to start a similar religious ceremony.

How did that long ago man know all this? He's left so little of himself behind to tell us. But it is obvious he knew, and knew precisely.

There are 14 such petroglyphs that interact with sun and shadow scattered about the park, too many to make all this coincidence.

Some of the petroglyphs mark the winter solstice, others mark the summer solstice. And others mark midway between the two, the equinox.

The Petrified Forest and the Painted Desert are windy, deserty places today. But they are among the most important paleontological sites in the western hemisphere. Just recently they discovered "Gertie" here, the world's oldest datable, articulated dinosaur. Gertie roamed about 100 million years before the first flowers and grasses. She was about the size of a large dog, and when Gertie was wandering about, the land was steamy, tropical, lush ferns waved in the breeze.

Those huge fern trees fell eventually, fell into the swamps. Gertie and those other, bigger creatures died and they, too, fell into the swamps and time passed and things changed and the swamps dried up and the land became a high desert. The Anasazi came, lived their lives, and left...

We don't know what the petroglyphs they left behind all mean. What the messages are. At least we didn't until Dr. Preston chanced on the solar happenings. Now, says Dr. Preston, "Maybe it's possible that the true meaning of the petroglyphs are just now coming to light, and what a fascinating story they might tell us about the people who created them."

Maybe...

Searcher among the stars

Covered with methane ice and circled by its giant solitary moon Charon, Pluto...the planet, not Mickey Mouse's dog...is somewhere around three BILLION miles out from our sun. So far away that no real picture has ever been taken of it other than what shows as a pinpoint of light in a crowd of millions of other pinpoints of light.

Generally, it is acknowledged that Percival Lowell, the founder of Lowell's Observatory in Flagstaff, made decisive contributions to astronomy that led to the discovery of Pluto. In the early 1900s Lowell began studying the orbits of Neptune and Uranus, then the farthest planets, and he discovered irregularities in their orbits leading him to believe that something was out there causing the irregularities. A Planet "X". Well, Lowell searched the heavens for this Planet "X", and unknowingly took pictures of it before he died. But Lowell's main love was his study of the planet Mars, and the search for Planet "X" fell to a young astronomer who would carry on the search for 14 years.

On March 3, 1979, I met Clyde Tombaugh at Lowell Observatory. It was Tombaugh who brought the announcement to the world on March 3, 1930, that a new planet had been discovered. Just fifty years later, we are standing and looking at a contraption that has lenses and mirrors and knobs and is really a sort of fancy slide viewer. It is the very device Clyde Tombaugh was using in 1930, to compare transparent photographic plates of millions of miles of space, when he detected one little wink of light that acted a little different from all the rest.

"And so you take two plates two nights apart within the same region. You compare one against another, back and forth." Tombaugh slides the transparencies into the viewing machine, one on each side. With a throw of a lever the right plate is illuminated in the view-finder, then the left. Each transparency is clear except for what appears to be thousands of black dots. The black dots are stars...

"Well, all together, counting the images on each plate which I had to see for a comparison, I saw, individually, ninety million star images over fourteen years. Sat at this for seven thousand hours."

"You looked at 90 million..."

"Saw every one of 'em..."

Well, he's dazzled me. I mean, 90 million black dots, "This must have been quite a discovery for the day. I mean, the 1930s, when things weren't quite so sophisticated..."

"Well, it was the first big planet discovery in several decades. You see, Neptune was discovered in 1846, and this (discovery of Pluto) was the first distant planet discovery since 1846."

The discovery was made on February 8, 1930, but the announcement was not made until almost a month later on March 13. For all the importance of the discovery of this new planet though, it turns out the heavens hadn't given up all that much of a secret. Pluto was too small to affect the orbits of Neptune and Uranus. There was still something out there they didn't understand, something that caused Neptune and Uranus to shift a little bit in their orbits.

Of course, I had to ask that standard question. "Do you think there is other life out there? Somewhere?"

"Our sun would surely not be so peculiar...since it's a fairly typical star...as to be the only one out of two hundred billion in our own galaxy to have a planet with intelligent life on it. And then, of course, there are billions of other galaxies made up of billions and billions of stars each one. So you see, there's an enormous range for all kinds of varieties of possibilities."

He holds up the plates with all the little black dots of stars among which, somewhere there, is Pluto.

"And I wouldn't be surprised that on even this pair of plates there are probably some stars, maybe a thousand, with planet systems with life of some kind on them."

Now that's kinda spooky, to think that out there among all those black dots there could be whole civilizations of intelligent beings. Fact and science fiction merging into a scattering of dots on a photo plate held in the hands of an old man who looked at them and looked at them, year after year, until he saw one little discrepancy, one little glitch in the order of things. A new planet.

Clyde Tombaugh, searcher among the stars. He found Planet "X".

A big meeting about the sky

Driving in to the south rim of the Grand Canyon that day in May of 1981, I was thinking, yuk, looks like it's going to rain. The horizon was heavy with rolling blackness, shafts of sunlight streamed down through breaks in the clouds, somebody up there shining monster, megawatt spotlights willy-nilly across the planet.

My assignment was to cover a conference at the canyon. They were calling it THE FIRST ANNUAL CONFERENCE ON THE SKY, and I was sure this was going to be one of those deals about pollution and smokestacks and maybe a few unkind words about jets flying over the Grand Canyon. I had already done one scary story here where they told me that, on some days, they were measuring smog from Los Angeles in the air over the canyon. On other days, when the wind shifted, they were measuring pollution from the smelter in Douglas and smelters in Mexico.

Glancing back up at the ominous, but what at least seemed to be pollution-free, sky, I thought, smog from Los Angeles in the Grand Canyon! Boy, we've gone too far!

But, it was not to be a conference about all that stuff. It was to be much more subtle.

For the next three days, people from all over the country would gather and they were going to talk about, THE SKY. And the big topic of discussion was going to be, do we really SEE the sky. Turns out, most of us really don't.

Jack Borden was the mastermind behind The Conference On The Sky. A fellow in his late thirties, medium height, medium build. Dark, curly hair with just a touch of gray. Good looking.

"People will say, 'what do you see in the sky that we don't see?' " Jack waved his hand at the heavens. "You look up there and we see a few clouds blowing by, maybe some blue, maybe some gray. But when you step into a more intimate awareness of the wonder of the sky. You look at it, and that's what you say, 'WOW!', I've been living under this for my whole life and I never really saw it before."

To do the interview, I set the camera right on the edge of the canyon, with all those ominous clouds rolling around in the background. Pretty clever, huh?

Jack Borden had been a television reporter, and spent all his life wandering around in wide open spaces and under wide open skies and never saw the sky until about a year ago.

"I was taking a snooze after a little hike with my wife and opened my eyes and BANGO, there it was! I saw the sky for the first time in my life. Following that I figured, hey, if I went that long in my life with all that exposure to wide vistas and skies and I had to wait that long to finally see it, I was gonna check out the rest of the people."

For a television story he covered the eyes of a few people on the street and asked them, what was in the sky that day? NOBODY could really tell him.

"So, we've just done a study with the University of Arizona. A professor there has gone to five different cities and talked to 675 people in those cities and asked them what the sky looked like outside. Less than 50 percent knew what they saw. Incredible.

"Ninety-seven percent of the people who were questioned were absolutely positive that their desription of the sky was accurate." Jack shakes his head in wonder. "This means that half the people in the world, or at least half the people in those cities, are walking around being absolutely positive about things that are absolutely wrong."

Are there any rules to watching the sky? Do you have to know what to look for?

"All kinds of things happening in the sky. There are sundogs, there are iridescent clouds, you got rainbows in the clouds going all day, you got shafts of light even in a gray sky. Look up there right now, you got beautiful folds in the clouds. And I'm not a meteorologist, a climatologist, I don't know anything about it. Hell, I don't know a cirrus cloud from a circus clown. I've almost consciously avoided all this terminology. I mean, listen, if I look at Bo Derek, for example, I don't have to know anything about physiology. To enjoy Bo Derek?"

We laughed. The man did have a point.

And the man had a point about the sky. I remembered another day I spent on the edge of this Grand Canyon, a day I was truly amazed by the sky. And a little frightened. Just at sunset a monster thunderstorm moved slowly across the canyon. Blinding streaks of lightning sizzled out of the black and down through curtains of rain and attacked the ground. Cracks of thunder so sharp and loud I involuntarily winced stunned the senses and rocketed through heavy air in rapid succession. Occasional pauses were filled with muted rumbling that rolled and bounced through the canyon, black threads of violence on the way.

As if to apologize and appease for all this incredible violence, the setting sun broke through in places and cast out splashes of intense reds and oranges to paint the long corridors of the canyon. The dying sun shining on spires and peaks jutting up off the canyon floor threw long, long shadows so black no mortal eye could pierce them. . .a display no mere man could ever equal.

Jack Borden was right. Here is a theater with ever changing acts of wonders, a panoramic stage of bedazzlement. The playground of the gods. Incredible energy and beauty. An amazing, free show that can be seen. . .from anywhere.

And we seldom just. . .look up!

Arm wrestling

Arm wrestling is a simple deal, right? Something you do at the ol' pub to sort of, friendly-like, show the other guy your macho. A just-below-the-surface sort of violence that articulates better than words, hey, I AM tougher than you are, old son. A muted display of physical power that establishes, however subtly, the manly pecking order for the evening, right now, right up front.

Well, maybe it's simple to you who have not been caught up in the competition of it all. The bulging muscle of it all, the flex and haughty stare of it all. The disdainful, superior squint one who has the big pecs can hurl down at lesser humans. Arm wrestling is also a place to learn one of life's basic truths...the hard way.

I wandered into MetroCenter in Phoenix one afternoon quite by accident looking for something, I don't remember what. In the center mall area there must have been 500 people stomping around, shouting, cheering. For the life of me I couldn't see what they were stomping and shouting and cheering about.

Suddenly, a horrible scream. AAARRRGHH!!! Another... AAARRRGGGHH!!

Up on a small stage two men faced each other. Two BIG men, HEAVILY muscled men. The screamer was a wild-eyed guy in bib overalls. He pounded the table, thrust out his chest and screamed at the guy across the table from him, trying to intimidate him. The other guy looked at the audience, smirked. The crowd loved it.

I ran out and got my TV camera. I had obviously run into some weird religious get-together...some pagan, ritualistic performance. Up on that stage we had religious objects: an altar-table with two stick-like objects in front of the two men. We had religious fervor: 500 folks shouting and weaving around. We had followers, the faithful: guys lined up waiting for their turn in front of the altar.

We had, folks, a gathering of...ARM WRESTLERS!

The High Priest (referee) checks that both followers are locked in ritualistic position: elbows on the table, hands legally gripping, free hands grabbing the sticks for support. Finally he's satisfied, steps back. "GO!"

A roar rumbles up out of the crowd. Shouts, screams.

The table trembles under the strain. The wrestlers' faces squinch, staring at each other from a foot apart, a quivery, malevolent glare. Muscles bunch, bulge, sweat glistens. Veins throb from the strain. The crowd stomps and yells, thirsting for blood. This could easily become a Roman Coliseum...only one contestant walking away!

Slowly, one arm begins a shuddering descent. The crowd smells defeat, stomping, clapping, chanting, "DOWN...DOWN... DOWN!!" PLOP! The hand slaps the table, the winner breaks away, throws both arms up in victory. The loser, he of big, but not big enough, muscles, slinks away. Macho punctured.

What we had here was not just a gathering of your Saturday afternoon, local bar, betcha-a-beer arm wrestlers. What we had here were big, mean, heavily-muscled, break-your-arm-for-fun arm wrestlers.

The event was the World Professional Arm Wrestling Association's Arizona Championships. Winners here went on to the world's finals. Can you imagine that if these guys are big, how big they must be at the world competition?

Anybody could enter. All you had to have was the six dollar entry fee. And enough muscles to knock a Greyhound bus unconscious.

I noticed some interesting things about basic human behavior at this event. There were some pretty big guys in the audience and I heard them talking about entering, bragging, flexing muscles, smiling archly at their girlfriends. But when the BIG guys showed up, and they saw some REAL muscles, they just sort of sat quietly in the audience, discreetly aware of a basic life truth: there is...ALWAYS...someone bigger and meaner than you are.

Except for maybe the guy I think won this event. The monster that ambled up to the table, smiling gently, was Ed Golian, middle-weight defending champion, and a doctor in Scottsdale. His opponent smirked at him. There's a lot of smirking at these events. Ed wiped the smirk off his opponent's face in one easy, piston-like stroke. WHAM! Ed Golian smiled easily, sort of a gosh-too-bad-fellow grin.

Whistles and catcalls now. The gal walking up to the table was pretty, shy. This was the women's division. Only eight entered and a couple of them were pretty tough and the winner was the hefty gal nobody whistled at when SHE walked up. The kind of gal who frightens big guys. She took the pretty gal's arm and slammed it on the table with a vengeance. The pretty gal winced in pain and wandered off. Lots of good lines to be written here but I'm probably going to get letters as it is.

And remember the screamer? The guy in bib overalls who thrust out his chest and let loose those wild-eyed screams at his opponent? AAARRRGHH!! It didn't do him any good. His opponent beat him. The screamer shambled off, realizing a basic life truth. There IS always someone out there who is bigger and meaner... remember?

Better believe it, folks.

Another cowboy gone

He was a cowboy.

Kind of an ol' bowlegged cowboy, an easy smile, and he liked an old, slow country waltz better than anything in the world.

He passed away last year at 90 years old and we lost another precious link in a terribly short chain connecting us to the past. At his 90th birthday party, several months before he died, he remarked, "You know folks, I'm just so proud to be here. At my age, damned if I ain't glad to be anywhere!"

It was a grand old surprise for Frank Trammell. A gathering of friends at the civic center in Black Canyon City. His wife, Rena, almost had to beat him up to get him out of the car and walk in to see what was going on. They had just come back from playing and singing at an affair down Phoenix way.

Anyone familiar with country and blue grass and fiddle and music in Arizona knew the Trammells. They showed up at all the events: the Payson Fall Fiddling Contest, the doings over at Wickenburg, everywhere anybody got together and put bow to fiddle, mouth to harmonica, strum to guitar. Rena played the guitar and sang; Frank played harmonica.

But, to appreciate Frank Trammell, you had to know that Frank was a cowboy. Born in West Texas in 1896, Frank was cowboying by the time he was ten years old.

The railroads came to West Texas in the 1880s, but it was about 1910 before they really got their act together and could supply enough equipment to load up and ship out all the cattle that ranchers sold to slaughter houses in the East.

Before the railroads came, there were the years of the long trail-drives between Texas and railheads in Kansas. They pretty much ended with the coming of the railroads, but not altogether. Up until about 1910 many west Texas cattlemen still drove their herds to Oklahoma and Kansas. Frank Trammell was on some of those last trail drives...

"I went on several trail drives from Texas up to Kansas and I remember goin' on one...there's a big blizzard all the way...rainy and freezin' and we just saddled up the horses and walked and hung onto their tails and drove 'em along..."

Frank and I and some other folks from the birthday party have come outside to sit under a tree and take some fresh air. Frank is sort of holding court and I'm video-taping him for a story I'm going to air...

"We had ice in the saddles, ice in our nose. Our bedrolls were frozen every night. Had beef and beans and sourdough biscuits three times a day. Some of them ol' trail cooks had sourdough starters they'd had going for 30 years...

"An' another thing. There wasn't no wood. Hell, that country was called, 'where the wind made the water and the cows cut the wood.' And that was it. There wasn't no wood in that country."

Several listeners are confused. Cows cut the wood? I knew what it meant, but I asked...

"How...what do you mean, the cows cut the wood?"

"We burned the cow chips."

"That's what I thought you meant."

Some of the listeners aren't sure their legs aren't being pulled. It's true, they burned cow chips.

"In all that rainy weather, we'd gather them things up, dry 'em out an' that's what we had to cook with. You didn't, you didn't eat!"

There's a twinkle in Frank's eye. "Sometimes them campfire beans had this funny taste...

"But cold? We had this ol' tent but the damn thing was all froze together and when we bent it, it broke. An' I could tell you more about what happened...well, we all got in this tent and there's one ol' boy must, uh...I don't know if I should tell you what happened..." Laughing, Frank looks over at a friend. His friend has obviously heard the story, he's laughing, says, ah, go ahead.

"Well, this one ol' boy had the BUGS. An we all were sleeping together there to keep warm, keep from freezin', and we all got 'em!"

After all these years he still looks disgusted about what happened, but he's trying hard to keep from laughing at his own story. I almost drop the TV camera.

"An' it was about two months 'fore we got back to the ranch and I tell you...them bugs is done a pretty good job on me!"

People are starting to wander out of the civic center wondering what all the hysterical laughter is about.

"In all that cold, how in the world did you sleep at night?" I asked.

"We didn't sleep. We just wallered around there. Yeah."

Laughter here blends with laughter a little bit later when Frank is asked to blow out the candles on the cake. They're trick candles and when you blow one out, it lights right back up again. Finally, Frank

is reduced to beating at the candles with his cowboy hat. "What the hell!"

"Frank, what's your favorite song?"

"Waltz Across Texas!"

It's pickin' and singin' time now. Rena and Frank are doing "Waltz Across Texas." Frank is blowin' on an old harmonica, Rena picks and sings...

It's a fairy land tale that's come true...
And with your hand in mine...
I could dance on and on...
I could waltz across Texas with you...

"We go out different places. I enjoy myself. I try to entertain other people. I like to entertain people. I like to make 'em laugh an' enjoy themselves. I get more kick outta that than anything."

It's been a good afternoon, a lot of good friends, a lot of good music.

"Bill, I lived a good clean life, worked hard. Never ex-ag-grated myself or browsed or cruised around too much. That's what I get for it. I thank the Lord I'm still stickin' around."

Somehow 90 years get by. Three years overseas in WWI, then back to being a cowboy. Met and married Rena in the 40s, moved to California where he was a cattle inspector, then came to Arizona. Spent his last years operating an old store in Black Canyon City and going out singing and playing every chance he got.

Rena looks fondly at her husband when she sings, "...and I can waltz across Texas...with you."

That afternoon wore down and a February sun dropped low in the sky. Folks began to leave. A hug, a kiss, a squeeze. I guess maybe there's something...something in the air that makes a fellow's eyes water up a bit. A fellow like ol' Frank Trammell, celebrating all those years. A nice, slow waltz across the memories.

* * *

A few months later we were all back at the same place. Frank had passed away. Rena was talking to me.

"This is the way my husband wanted it to be. 'Nothing too fussy or too churchy. Just let me hear some good ol' gospel singers and bring in some fiddlers and have some playing and singing,' he said. 'I don't want nobody to feel that this is a bad time. I'm going to a better place.'"

They played Tennessee Waltz.

"He was a super person. I had him 41 years and I don't regret any of them. But I wouldn't call him back. He's in a better place now."

There was some good ol' gospel singing.

And there was something...something in the air. Made the eyes water up a bit.

An ol' sad fiddle, soft strains in the quiet room, Waltz Across Texas...

Ah, hell, I'll just admit it to you. I cried.

Canyon de Chelly

The Navajo mother is sick and tired of her children being bad and disobedient and uncontrollable. So she travels up the canyon to Speaking Rock, looks up and yells, "Hey, Speaking Rock! Tell Spider Woman my children are being bad!"

According to Johnny Guerro, Speaking Rock then turns to Spider Rock...Spider Woman lives up on top...and tells her about the bad children. "So many people come here and start looking at this rock and they say...'man, how'd this rock get this name...it don't look like no spider?'" Johnny Guerro was our guide in Canyon de Chelly. Johnny claims to be half Navajo, half Apache, half White Man, half this and that.

"Well, it's the old Navajo traditional story that Spider Woman lives on top...this is a way of correcting children...they tell the kids that Spider Woman has all these big, black spiders on this rock and they spin these webs around this rock formation to the canyon floor. And, when these kids get bad...well, Spider Woman'll send down her big, black spiders who'll pick up these bad children...and they take 'em on top of Spider Rock and eat 'em up there. 'Cause, on top of that rock is a white cap...that represents all the bleached bones of those bad children the spiders ate up there."

It is not the world's deepest canyon, or the longest, and there is not a famous river running through it to the sea. But Canyon de Chelly weaves its own special spell on people. It is a canyon of sheer cliffs and twists and turns and sudden reminders of other civilizations. Round a turn and up on a ledge in the cliff, the ruins of an Anasazi dwelling.

It is a canyon where heroes of childhood once walked, not so gloriously as we might have wished, though. Kit Carson rounded up surrendering Navajos here and took them on the infamous LONG WALK in 1864. Took them to a desolate place in New Mexico called Bosque Redondo...so different from their canyon home.

It is a canyon of spirits and ghosts and stories. It is a canyon considered by many to be even more impressive, more magnificent than the Grand Canyon. One can hardly wind their way up the canyon, beneath towering sandstone cliffs that rise, at times, 1000 feet straight up...sheer faces that look like they were carved by some impressionistic giant wielding a monster putty knife...and not be impressed. After the giant smeared on the sandstone icing, he then decorated the cliff faces with patina streaks (water from millions of years of thundershowers, running down the cliffs, drying on the heated rock, drawing up mineral material to the surface, coating into a patina stain called "desert varnish").

Canyon de Chelly is a National Monument on the Navajo Reservation near Chinle, in the northeastern part of Arizona. It is a rugged repository of over a 1,000 years of occupation, first by the Anasazi, more recently by the Navajos. Navajo families still live in Canyon de Chelly.

Visitors to Canyon de Chelly may not go into the canyon without a guide. Most visitors take a half or full day tour provided by Thunderbird Lodge at Chinle, and they go into the canyon with a Navajo guide driving a four-wheel drive truck with open-air seats. But, individual guided trips can be arranged. There are at least two good reasons why you have to have a guide: the guides help you respect the privacy of the Navajo families who live in the canyon; and they make sure you aren't the victim of a very real, substantial danger in the canyon...quicksand.

After rainstorms, lots of water runs down the canyon and the saturated sand becomes treacherous with pockets of quicksand. Pockets big enough to swallow cars and trucks whole. More than a dozen vehicles have disappeared in the sands here.

"In 1979 there was a '76 Chevrolet truck buried right in there." We are sloshing along barefooted in the stream at the bottom of the canyon listening to Navajo guide Wilson Hunter. He is guiding a group from the Museum of Northern Arizona on a day-long hike. "They tried to dig it out, but...you can imagine another 100 years or so some archeologist digging it out and trying to name that site. What do you think they'll call it?"

There are several guesses. "Chevrolet #47. Chevrolet Site?."

"Well, I'd call it 'Canyon de Chevy' wouldn't you?"

A hearty round of boos and hisses. But, a very real danger.

There is one hike you can make into Canyon de Chelly without a guide, that's down from the rim on the White House trail to White House ruins. It's a little over a mile on a well-marked trail and it takes you to one of the better known Anasazi sites in Canyon de Chelly.

" 'Course the Anasazi people...that's what the Navajo call these people...the 'ancient ones' who have gone on before us...we know very little of them." Johnny Guerro points up at the impressive structure that housed generations of Anasazi for almost 300 years. "They lived in this canyon the year round and they always lived on this north side to utilize the sun in the winter time. The buildings standing here were built anywhere from 1000 to about 1280 AD."

By 1300, archeologists believe, the Anasazi were gone from Canyon de Chelly, and from the area. The canyon fell silent.

*　*　*

The man walking down the bottom of Canyon de Chelly is barefooted, sloshing along through the stream. He's an older gentleman, in his late sixties. He has a smile on his face.

"What are you learning from this little trek?" I asked him.

He laughs. "It's fun to walk in the mud again. I haven't walked in the mud for 60 years." It is a pleasant walk down a pleasant, quiet place in this world. The pleasures of life can be simple ones.

He's part of a group of folks (all of whom are barefooted and splashing along like kids) on a four-day tour of Navajo country. The tour was sponsored by the Museum of Northern Arizona and on this day they have hired Navajo guide Wilson Hunter to lead them on a wandering trek down off the rim of Canyon de Chelly, then down the canyon to its mouth. They will pass old Anasazi ruins, petroglyphs, Navajos herding sheep. They will pass through centuries of time.

Laura Graves Allen is along, she's an anthropologist with the museum. "This is a walk with someone who can answer questions like, 'what's that over there?' We try to help them look for the subtle things. I think once they start knowing where to look and what they're looking for, it's a lot easier for them to go on a hike like this on their own."

Steve Guyer came from the plains of Texas to join this tour. "I think it's good to kinda' get off and try to feel all this silence. If you can feel the silence, you can feel the immensity of the canyon, and perhaps the significance that it's been...not only to the Navajo who are living here today...but the ancient people who lived here in the past."

We leave the museum group and head on up canyon. As we leave, Wilson Hunter is showing the folks how to eat certain parts of a cactus. I thought, this is where you'd better pay attention. Better know which is the right part to be eating.

Around a bend we visit a place most folks don't get to go, Planetarium Ruin. Here, another surprise left by folks gone for centuries now, a small ruin in a cleft at the bottom of a patina-stained cliff. It's almost a cave.

Johnny points up. "On the ceiling of this cave right here, black X's and black X's with circles around them, made with charcoal.

People who study the stars have taken pictures of these and actually lined them up with our present day solar system." A tantalizing facet of a long-gone people. What were they doing here, studying the stars?

Down below us we hear the clanking of a bell. "Sheep," says Johnny. "Looks like ol' Tom Deadman down there."

Navajos have lived in Canyon de Chelly for hundreds of years. Tom Deadman walks through a scene that is as old as Navajos. Sheepherding. We go down and walk along with Tom and his flock of sheep. He speaks English and we learn that herding sheep is simpler than you might expect. All you have to know are a few special phrases. A couple of sheep fall behind.

Tom yells a special sheepherding command. "RUN!!"

The two sheep look up, startled, then break into a shambling run and catch up with the rest of the flock.

Tom looks at the sheep sternly. "Yeah...they understand me."

On up the canyon, past places...

"This big, black desert varnish patina stain coming over the cliff...the old Navajo legend is that a Ye'i...that means like a giant, or a Ye'i-so (pronounced yay-eet-so), a big scary person, was killed up on top of the mesa at this point, and the stain is the blood as it runs over the side of the cliff from this murdered giant." As Johnny Guerro tells us this legend, I look up at the desert varnish spilling off the cliff top. It makes sense.

Traveling up past old places now, sad places. An old hogan, a hole busted through the west wall. Nobody's lived here for a hundred years.

"It's been abandoned and the reason is because of the old traditional religious...superstitious...belief that when someone dies in a hogan, they leave it and never go back. And the old traditional way is, they will knock a hole in the west end of the hogan so the spirit can leave."

Navajos say, don't go inside one of these hogans, bad spirits still there might hitch a ride out...on your soul.

"People come here and feel a feeling." Johnny Guerro searches for the right words. "They feel something. A spirit. Sometimes it's almost religious, they say. That's the way of Canyon de Chelly."

Canyon de Chelly. A place of stories and legends...and all those spirits moving about. The count of men and years and canyon here ticks back for thousands of years. Come here and walk through. Let the canyon wash over your soul. It surely will.

The F-15 Flight

I walked into the headquarters building of the 555th Eagle Triple-Nickle) Squadron on Luke Air Force Base. I was starting he process that would, if only for a few minutes, put me at the ontrols of one of the world's most sophisticated jet fighters, the ʰ-15.

Now, you don't just walk in and hop into an F-15 and roar off nto the wild blue yonder. Press orientation flights are handed out vith a great deal of stinginess, and to reporters who either report .bout aviation, or who are pilots themselves and can translate the lying experience to a wide audience. Three hours of briefing before ʰou head out on the flight line are intense and serious.

Mostly the instructions center around what to do should you ιave to bail out. I kidded around a little bit at first, but the Air ʰorce Captain assigned to lead me through all this gave me a look hat said, this isn't a joke. I got serious, I wanted to fly in this .irplane.

The lady in the Air Force fatigues was pleasant, but rough. She inched the G-suit on like a victorian corset. "It's kinda like getting nto one of those corsets..."

Another lady pulled a helmet down over my ears. An angry-ʲoking eagle was painted on the helmet, and the numbers "555."

"Are your ears in the cup all the way? Otherwise you won't hear ιnything."

"I can't hear you," I shouted.

Helmet on, G-suit cinched up, flight boots on. In front of a nachine with an oxygen mask, which she places over my nose and nouth. "Take a deep breath and hold it, I'm going to take you up to ⊦1."

She clicked in 41 on the dial, I held my breath. Nothing ιappened.

"Fine." She smiled and clicked me back to zero. I'm not sure vhat we did there.

The Captain again and I'm in the cockpit of an F-15 simulator. ʰNow let's say you have an emergency on the ground. You have to accomplish an emergency ground egress, which means you have to get your own self out of the airplane, because the pilot will be makin' tracks himself." For some reason this strikes the serious Captain as funny and he laughs.

Now I'm strapped into the parachute simulator, hanging a foot or so off the floor. The Captain is serious again.

"Now, Mr. Leverton, the signal to eject is when the pilot yells at you, 'BAIL-OUT! BAIL-OUT!' If you're still in the airplane on the third time he yells bail-out . . . you're flying solo!" This also strikes Captain Serious as funny.

Now fully clothed as a jet fighter pilot, and walking like I just spent a week on horseback, we all meet in a briefing room. My escort and fellow pilot during the day would be Major Darrell Smith of the Triple-Nickle Squadron.

"And what we want to do is take it to mild, basic fighter maneuvers," his left hand is flying slightly behind his right hand in a tight left turn, "where we'll end up behind the other aircraft and we'll practice shooting our radar missiles as we come in behind him." His left hand vibrates as make-believe missiles launch out toward his right hand. "We'll practice some air combat to arrive at a guns-tracking-kill solution on the number two aircraft. Not for combat aircraft." (Remember now, the F-16 had not yet arrived on Air ton." Everybody laughs politely. However, his right hand is spiraling toward the floor in flames.

Finally, waddling along like a duck out of water, it was time to go flying!

"Well, it's the finest airplane in the United States Air Force invenventory." The Commander of the squadron walked along the rows of F-15s with us. "It's probably the world's most capable aircraft." (Remember now, the F-16 had not yet arrived on Air Force Force flight lines when I took this ride). There's no question we have pushed technology to the limits with modern-day airplanes. When I was a youngster, I read Flash Gordon, and now I'm just about flying what Flash Gordon had at that time.

Walking along the rows of parked F-15s I get the definite impression of silent, sulking monsters. Some great, gray, fast bird of prey perched, hunched over, waiting for an enemy rabbit or mouse to wander unsuspecting by . . .

Strapped into the rear seat. Major Smith in the front seat. The twin jet engines spool up to power. The F-15 rumbles and ticks and things go beep in the headset and we vibrate and it seems to be

straining at the leash. We taxi out.

Take-off was a real screamer! A maximum-performance take-off with after-burners, one hell of a roar and a hard shove into the back of the seat and my body trying desperately to catch up with the plane. We lift off, wheels thump into the wings, and when three-hundred-miles an hour is reached, and reached quickly, Major Smith pulls gently back on the controls and into a sixty-degree climb to 17,000 feet! He pulls the F-15 over on its back which places us on a southerly heading. We roll over right-side-up.

Off our left wing Captain Bud Temples slides up beside us in a single-seat F-15. Both of us fly south to the Air Force's Gila Bend Gunnery Range. Separating, we go south, Captain Temples goes north. Once in position, we try to find Captain Temples on the F-15's super-sophisticated radar system and make a simulated launch of missiles at him. The launches will be recorded on a computer and later Major Smith and Captain Temples will be able to tell how accurate they were.

"We're trying to get a heat-seeking missile off. And...fox-one ("fox-one" means he has fired one missile)! I got a tally-ho on the target."

It's hard to describe what the F-15's computer will do. What it won't do might be easier. It won't cook breakfast, but it will guide you around the sky at incredible speeds and fight a battle with other aircraft anywhere within a hundred miles ...you can actually shoot down another aircraft and never see him with the naked eye. If you don't feel up to dealing personally with the enemy, push a button and the plane does it for you.

Not sure where you are? Or how to get where you're going? The computer will figure it out for you and place you within a city block of where you want to be. And if you don't mind the fuel bill, it can all be done at two and a half times the speed of sound.

Now that we've shot at Captain Temples and presumably eliminated him from our mock battle, it's time to fool around a little bit.

In a maximum-G turn the blood rushes away from my brain and leaves me looking down a long, black tunnel at a pin-point of light in my mind and my cheeks wrap up around my ears.

We rocket through the speed of sound, almost a thousand miles an hour.

Major Smith let me take the controls and we chased Captain Temples through the rarified air of 40,000 feet. I tried a roll, a loop, an immelmann. We punched through the top of a thunderhead at 600 miles an hour. GOD! What fun! Master of the sky! Me at the controls of the most sophisticated aircraft in the world! It was over all too soon.

All the other stuff was anti-climactic, back to Luke, shake hands, receive a framed picture with patches that proclaimed me an Eagle Driver. And talk about, and talk about, and I'm still talking about, that F-15 flight.

Cafes on the Arizona Road

I get asked a lot, "Where do you eat out there ON THE ARIZONA ROAD? You must get some pretty bad food!" Well, sometimes I do, but I've discovered there are places to eat that kinda get lost in the freeway rush and high tech roar of 20th Century living. I want to tell you about them because I'm afraid they are a part of a vanishing American scene. Verses we forget the words to in an old American Waltz.

* * *

Sleet and wind and mist whistled through the open door where the cowboy stood stomping mud from his boots.

"You gonna leave that damn door open all day, you dumb cowboy?" waitress Linda shouted over her shoulder as cold air swirled across the room.

The tall cowboy, a little sheepish, dripping wet, eased the door shut. "Sorry, Linda, I jus' din't wanna mess up your floor." If the cowboy had taken offense, he could have broken every bone in Linda's body with a casual flick of a hand.

The streets of this small, southeastern Arizona farming town are empty. The frosty windows of the cafe rattle occasionally from a freezing December wind filled with spattering sleet. Merle Haggard is on the jukebox singing as to how he'll be just one more love that some gal can dream about 'cause he'll be gone. Several men at a table are drinking coffee, laughing. The room is a bright oasis of warmth in a gray, sloshy world.

"Well, git in here and git some coffee down ya. Doncha have any sense to come in outta' all that?" She pours coffee and pats the cowboy affectionately on the head.

At the other table one of the men hollers, "Hell, Linda, that's the only reason he come in here at all, to ask somebody what all that wet stuff on his head is..."

I had wandered in a few minutes before, beat down by miles and miles of bad roads and bad weather and was having a hamburger. I was listening to a conversation that would never take place at a

McDonald's. And, I thought, what was going on here made a good point about places like this little cafe. It could . . . be just a place to eat . . . like McDonald's.

But it happens that cafes have personalities to go along with the serving of food . . . and I for one am glad they do. And beatin' down a lot of Arizona blacktop every year, I'm glad there are these warm places to hole up in a bit and shake off the road and the chill and grab a bite to eat. Places where it's OK to linger.

Places they call . . . CAFE.

So, next time you're rolling down some ol' long Arizona Road and it gets time to knock back the hungries, try a cafe. You might discover a special place.

Now, there are ways to tell if you're in a real cafe. Most real cafes are out in the country somewhere and are painted white and the sign says "Cafe." But there are exceptions. So be careful, be alert.

Inside, it is not only socially correct but almost socially necessary to have signs on the wall that suggest you not be critical of the cook. Or the food. Or the waitress. Or John Wayne. Or America.

And, if the menu sort of resembles what your mother's entire culinary repertoire was for a month, you're probably in a good cafe. There should be stuff on the menu like fried chicken, chicken fried steak, liver and onions, pork chops, biscuits and gravy, bacon and eggs, pancakes. If there's something on the menu you can't pronounce, you probably ought to smile, check your watch and get back out on the ol' blacktop. Something serious has happened here and what cafes are all about has begun to fade from the place.

Fade. That's a nice word for what's happening. Cafes are fading from the American Scene. And it is, I submit, because we go too fast. It is no longer time-effective, or even psychologically very comfortable, to sit down and get face-to-face with . . . A STRANGER . . . and munch our way through a few forced moments of sociability. We are ALL strangers out there, ALL mobile, fleet of foot, looking straight ahead, march-stepping down a fast-food line, gastronomically red-lined in 90 seconds or our money back.

I'm not suggesting that the food at a cafe is going to be better than anywhere else, but there's a good chance it will be. And more of it, and cheaper. But you'll have to pay the price. You'll have to sit a few minutes . . .

I guess it's a nostalgia thing with me. It hurts my feelings. I'm not opposed to change. Like the guy said in an article I read: "It doesn't bother me that gas stations don't check my oil anymore, or even pump the gas. I don't care there aren't any more dime stores or corner barbershops or nickel cups of coffee or things like that. But the waning number of cafes definitely defines an erosion of America."

So, cafes can't really compete with the 20th century. They just don't have advertising dollars and they can't survive freeways passing them by. But the cafe hasn't vanished entirely, and in Arizona, there are some cafes of note.

* * *

I gotta' tell you, there are just some things you can't get at Jack-In-The-Box.

Like what you get at Mary's Cafe out on Highway 89 just south of Winona Road in Flagstaff. . .food at a place that's famous all over northern Arizona as much for Mary as for the food. The little white cafe on the east side of the road has been there for 23 years and Mary Lund has been there for 23 years and things are done just a certain way and they've always been done that way and they always will.

They cut their own meat and grind their own hamburger, make all their own sauces, gravies, soups and cut and mash the potatoes. They even candy the yams themselves.

The menu is cafe all the way and don't expect anything fancy, but there will be plenty of it, and it will be good food at a good price.

Mary Lund is a slight, thin woman of indeterminate age who is well-liked by her regulars, many of whom have been coming here for ten, fifteen, twenty years. Mary is known, however, to launch healthy verbal attacks on any truck driver who looks like he's been driving too long, or any local official whose political bent differs from hers and who wanders innocently in for lunch. Other regulars, on an apparent indiscriminate and indeterminate schedule, will find themselves biting into a rubber hamburger, or looking up into the path of a "runaway" cream pie. One can only guess it's true when Mary states: "I've caught a few myself."

A sign on the wall declares, "This is a high class place, act respectable." A poster of John Wayne hangs in a prominent spot.

"I believe in being just down-to-earth and honest and bulling with the customers. Make it as much like home as it can be," Mary says.

Mary's Cafe is open 24 hours a day, seven days a week. There are specials every day at lunch and supper: chicken and dumplings, barbecued ribs, meat loaf . . .

I had breakfast there one morning and the waitress called me "honey" at least 48 times, which usually aggravates me, but this gal had an easy way about her that made it OK. At least one of the waitresses there will rub the tired kinks out of your shoulders if you're one of the regulars and if she has the time. I hear it's worth coming in when she has time.

You don't get that at McDonald's.

But what you do get at the Four-B's Cafe in Black Canyon City is more for less than you do anywhere else. This is one of those places, like Mary's, where truckers stop because of the food and not because the waitresses are prettier or there is sufficient room to park their big rigs. It's hard to park a big rig at the Four-B's, so they have to WANT to eat here.

Outwardly, the Four-B's Cafe qualifies for what Madison Avenue would call regressive advertising. It is NOT impressive. A white building about 30 feet by 30 feet. The kitchen is a tiny, hot, sizzling trap . . . black grill on one side, sinks and a little counter space on the other and a chopping table separating the two. A sign over the entrance to the kitchen warns, "If you can't wait, don't order!" which is misleading because, normally, the service is fast.

Since seating is at a premium, don't expect to have a table all to yourself, a lot of the tables are shoved together to save space. If you

The Four B's proprietors

can't stand company, this is not the place for you. The possibilities of who might share your lunch-space here are mind-boggling. Truckers, travelers, highway patrolmen, kids, bikers, shifty-eyed strangers. It's a good place to hear an opinion other than your own. Or maybe keep yours to yourself.

The Four-B's are Boyd, Bessie, Bill and Betty, the owners. They sort of fell into the cafe business back in 1979, a business none of them really knew anything about and Boyd says, "We just started putting out what looked right and it worked, so we didn't change anything."

What looks right to them would make restaurant operators elsewhere have a coronary. And has sent customers scurrying out to their cars to get the family Polaroid to take pictures of.

Be VERY CAREFUL ordering here. Especially at breakfast. A "stack" of pancakes flops over the edge of a regular-size plate, and if you order a side of sausage you will get a 10-to-12-ounce patty almost 8 inches in diameter. Bacon and eggs gets 6 or 7 pieces of bacon, and ham and eggs a massive slab of ham it will be hard to get through. Most folks don't finish what they order, which would seem to be a waste of food. But what you don't eat goes out the back door and is sold as...yes...pig feed.

Bill laughs. "I suppose if we knew anything about portions and running a business and all that stuff...it wouldn't work."

"We pay the bills," Boyd said.

Open 6 am to 9 pm daily, except Monday when they close at 3 pm, the Four-B's is a social gathering place and a place to get a whomping good meal at a good price.

Word gets around and the Four-B's has its cult following. Weekends are sort of "good-luck" days at the Four-B's. Everybody out for the weekend stops for breakfast and lunch and supper and in-between. It's not unusual, say, to see 50 motorcycles (no, not Hell's Angels) parked out front, people standing around waiting to get in, and motorcyclists inside expediting their own meals by helping the waitresses bus tables. The locals don't come around much on the weekends, they grumble a little about it, but other days it's a good place to come and fill up and visit a while.

* * *

At Lillie's Cafe in Bisbee you can get frog legs. That doesn't seem like a legitimate cafe menu item, but you have to remember that

Lillie comes from Arkansas and she KNOWS how to cook them. Even if all she can get around here are them little bitty frozen kind and Lord only knows where they caught the little buggers.

Folks at the Courthouse and construction workers and truck drivers and a gaggle of little old ladies heading for their weekly bridge party eat here and the door slammed open and one of those little old ladies popped in and yelled, "How ya' today, Lillie?"

Lillie is a large woman, short gray hair, glasses, who sits at her corner "office" table and keeps track of the comings and goings when she's not back in the kitchen cooking.

"I'm a-doing!" Lillie hollers back, then returns her attention to me. "Seven years ago a friend of mine had the place and he was going under. They'd cut off the electricity and I told him I didn't want it, but he pitched me the keys and walked off."

The table of bridge players is filling up. "Lillie, can I get a hamburger?"

Lillie and Ray

"Just hold your horses now, I'm talking to this big-city reporter. He's gonna' make me famous." The bridge player rolled her eyes and one of Lillie's noon-time waitresses hurried over to take her order.

"Everybody said I'd never make it," Lillie continued. "But I always figured that if I just served ol' country cookin' like the family did at home, it'd go over. And it did." She shrugs. "It's a place to spend my time."

Besides the regular menu, which has all the regular cafe stuff, there's a list of the day's specials on the wall. When she runs out of something, it gets erased. A bowl of beef stew that you need a goodly hunger to get around, roast pork, chicken and dumplings, cornbread everyday (you get cornbread everyday in Arkansas), Bar-B-Q ribs and big servings ("I got hungry folks coming in here") and reasonable prices and a worried look on Lillie's face if you don't clean your plate ("Didn't you like it?"). And frog legs.

For dessert there's plenty of home-baked stuff to choose from, including strawberry-rhubarb pie.

Located south of the circle in Bisbee on Highway 92 at the Naco Highway, Lillie's Cafe is just a tiny place you have to be alert to find, an old, white building much longer than it is wide. It's open Mon-Fri, 11 am to 6:45 pm, "If I don't get pooped out," and closed Saturday, and then open Sunday 11 to 3 for the church crowd.

The inside is neat as a pin and full of a crazy mixture of tempting, delicious smells emitting from the kitchen at the back. Lillie's husband, Ray, as thin as Lillie is large, works behind the scenes and doesn't say much except to ask me if I want to wash some pots and pans.

You don't get that at the Sonic Drive-In.

At "Rosie's Place", El Arte de Rosita, in Tucson you do get home cooked Mexican food in "Rosie original" surroundings. Year-round Christmas lights are strung all over the place and there is an ever-changing display of bric-a-bracs Rosita Fimbres gathers on her periodic trips to Mexico.

The place used to be just around the corner and used to be called El Chaparral. For 16 years El Chaparral was located in Ted De Grazia's studios on Campbell at Prince, and De Grazia and his cornies often gathered in a back corner to shoot the breeze. A picture of Rosita and De Grazia, which shows an obviously affectionate relationship, hangs in a prominent spot.

After De Grazia's death, the heirs wouldn't renew her lease and Rosita's clientele, all who apparently border on the fanatic, raised such a clamor that she managed to get a place just behind where she'd been. Turn east on Prince and immediately turn right into the church parking lot. It's OK to park there.

Rosita went into business 20 years ago in a little hole-in-the-wall place in downtown Tucson with a divorce and a ten dollar bill in

Rosita Fimbres with photo of Ted De Grazia

her hands. As soon as one customer paid, Rosita took that money out the back door to the nearest store, bought a head of lettuce or a pound of cheese and rushed back to get the next order out.

Rosita doesn't have a liquor license, but the people still come and that should tell you something about the food. People do bring their own booze and Rosita will bring a bucket of ice to the table.

Open 11 am to 9 pm Tues-Sat, service is friendly and reasonably prompt. In busy times the wait can seem pretty long, but nice things don't always come with the snap of a finger. Toni Fimbres, Rosita's daughter, sniffed, "If you want pre-fab food...go to Pancho's." I don't know where Pancho's is, but I suggest the trip wouldn't be worth it. And your order would be ready long before you got back.

Rosita at 65 is a constant, hovering presence. "I ain't gonna be no old lady!" She pretends she speaks only Spanish, but she told me that in English.

You don't get that at Taco Bell.

But you do get a sad feeling at the dying cafe in this one dusty little town I passed through.

A "For Sale" sign in the window. Fading John Wayne posters on the wall. Cracked vinyl on the booths. Pies store-bought. Trying too hard with the menu, things like malted waffles on the menu. Malted waffles?

Ah, fading away...

And I submit it's a shame, but that's the way it is, so I suggest you search around and find a good cafe and enjoy it in the time it has left. When Mary and the Four-B's and Lillie and Ray and Rosita all fade away, nobody's going to pick up where they left off. Except McDonald's and those guys. Yech.

*   *   *

I shot pictures of Ray and Lillie Green outside their tiny cafe. Walking back inside, Ray, a Texas boy, paused at the door, shook his finger at me.

"Now, Bill, you just tell 'em all we do is cook ol' country-style..."

It's getting to where you can't get that anymore.

Riding on the train, a last romance

When I was about 15 years old I lived for a while on the mainline of the Southern Pacific Railroad. I remember the rising thunder, the approaching rumble of the huge black steam engines swaying down the tracks, the rise and fall of the whistle, the incredible jolt through my heart as the train literally shook the earth and shook my bones and roared by, steel wheels pounding steel rails.

Then the fade of the engine dissolving to the steady, rhythmic beat of boxcars and clickety-clack of wheels and swirl of dust and wind and old pieces of paper and smoke and heat and then the caboose goes by and the noise and fury fades away, swallowed up by all that distance way down the tracks out of sight. That train headed for some faraway, romantic place that I wished, Lord, how I wished, I was going!

What a rush! to this day I still stop and watch a train go by. There is still something out of childhood that sees in a train a rumbling magic that can take me, swaying and clacking, off to some special place.

So, every now and then I succumb to that childhood romance with the rails and climb aboard a train and let it take me on down the line to look for that place. I can only tell you it is elusive, this mystery place, lost off somewhere in the heat waves where shimmering rails come together and the red light at the back of the train wavers . . . blinks . . . and is gone. Lord only knows where that mystery place is. I've never found it, but I KNOW it's out there. And I keep looking.

My wife, Bonnie, and I rode Amtrak's Sunset Limited out of Phoenix down to New Orleans. We bought a deluxe bedroom on one of the Superliner cars. We were to meet our friends Gene and Juanita Price in the Crescent City when the train arrived at 7:45 p.m. The plan was to go out to dinner and cruise the French Quarter until at least dawn and soak up, so to speak, a little of the flavor of New Orleans.

We were late. We didn't arrive in New Orleans until almost three in the morning. To make it even more embarrassing, Gene is the Southern District Supervisor for Amtrak. But it wasn't Amtrak's fault this time. There was a derailment on the Southern Pacific tracks that blocked the train.

But we eventually left Phoenix, rolling across the countryside. Amtrak's superliner equipment is modern, the deluxe bedrooms have private bathrooms, even a shower. Just don't mistake the shower button for the button that flushes the toilet or you're in for a real surprise. Ask Bonnie.

In what they call the "heyday" of passenger trains, the Sunset Limited was THE train, was THE role-model for other trains to imitate. Of course, passenger train service declined and deteriorated as more and more Americans got in their cars and on fast, efficient airlines and went those ways to all the places the train used to take them. When Amtrak took over the nation's aging fleet of 1920s and 30s and 40s passenger cars, the horror stories that came out of those first few years would curl your toes and make it seem almost suicidal to take the train.

Gradually, with whopping federal subsidies, Amtrak got their act together, replaced old cars with spanking new Superliner cars, took the best of the old cars and refurbished them, and nowadays run respectably close to being on time in comfortable equipment.

Tucson, Benson, Lordsburg, El Paso. Rolling, swaying gently along, countryside drifting by. Bonnie and I brought a little ice chest with drinks and snacks. Bonnie's propped up on the couch, sewing. I'm leaned back in the chair, feet up, trying to watch the late afternoon roll by. I drift in and out of sleep.

Brad Bowers, Amtrak's onboard chief, bursts into the compartment. This guy is constantly cheerful and somehow stays impeccably turned out in suit and tie, although he is probably up during most of the trip from Los Angeles to New Orleans. Brad is in charge of everything on the train except the actual running of the train itself. If you have a complaint, Brad is the person they'll send along to see you.

"Well, we're still only six hours behind schedule! Heck, we might even make up most of it by New Orleans."

"Relax, Brad. Have a snack."

"Yeah, well, not a chance, but I believe in being optimistic."

I personally don't care if we never get there. I'm riding the train because I want to be ON the train. And I found a lot of people on the train who felt that way. Mostly people were going someplace they wanted to get to, but the train was something they wanted to experience.

The man in the military uniform just doesn't like airplanes. "This is a lot more pleasant. On an airplane you get shoved on, strapped in, fed a drink and fed bad food and don't really have time to talk to anyone."

The lady playing solitaire was riding for the experience. For her it was a one-time deal and unfortunately she had been shuffled from car to car while Amtrak made up their mind about how best to move equipment around the derailment. The train was late, and she wound up in one of the older cars after she had paid for Superliner service. She would get a part of her money back, but the good feelings she wanted just weren't there.

"Bill, we do get a lot of people who ride for the nostalgia." It's night out now. Brad and I are sitting at a table in the empty dining car. Lights streak by outside. "But we get a lot of people who just want to be comfortable, relaxed. There are folks who are afraid to fly.

"Every form of transportation is subsidized. Taxpayers subsidize the airlines with control towers and airports and air traffic control systems. Highways are subsidized with gasoline taxes. Public transportation is never profitable, but we have to move certain segments of the population around."

Brad waves off in the direction of the world outside our speeding train. "Someday we're going to max out with cars and trucks and choke to death in our own smog. Amtrak and things like it are all going to be a matter of what we want . . ."

We train into the cities and towns through their backdoors, scratching along their underbellies. Clickety-clacking past back yards, junk yards, freight yards, grave yards. Under freeways, horn wailing almost constantly for the crossings, cars waiting, drivers tapping the wheel impatiently, rise and fall of the ding-ding-ding of crossing bells, dogs yap furiously, backsides of factories drift by.

Except at those stations where the engines have to be refueled, the train stops only a few minutes, sometimes just long enough for a passenger to step off. Most train stations are sad, run-down buildings in sad, run-down parts of town. There are exceptions. El Paso and San Antonio have renovated their stations. But mostly, off-track facilities are fading memories of what they used to be.

Really moving across south Texas now, 70 mph, gently rolling hills, forests, rivers, long shadows play out in front of a setting sun, our second evening on the train. At this very minute, gazing out the window, I am content with my place in the world. I have found a little bit of the magic . . .

But outside this rocketing cocoon of folks high-balling into a Texas night, there is a raging debate about whether we should continue to subsidize Amtrak or not. As good or bad as Amtrak might be, we have trapped ourselves in a deal it might cost more than it's worth to get out of.

De-funding Amtrak, according to Amtrak President W. Graham Claytor, Jr., would cost billions. "Three hundred million would have to be paid immediately in severance payments and other employee benefits," Claytor told the Associated Press. "If Amtrak went out of business it would have to pay 2.1 billion dollars over six years to 21,000 displaced workers. There wouldn't be enough money from liquidating assets to pay mandated labor settlements.

"You have generated a liability that leaves you under water. It's going to cost the government more money to get rid of Amtrak than it is to keep it going."

Past midnight now, the Sunset Limited crosses bayous in Louisiana, anchor lights on fishing boats ghosting by, rippling reflections in the water. Up, over and down the Huey P. Long Bridge spanning the Mississippi River.

Amtrak is probably here to stay. Gene Price, who met us at the New Orleans station is convinced that Amtrak will eventually pay its own way.

"Trains are still popular, Bill." Our train had backed into a dead-end track that ends at the doors to the New Orleans station. "No Congressman wants to tell his constituents the train won't be running through their hometown. We have a good image, we're non-polluting, safe, cheap."

Gene and Bonnie and Brad and I wandered over to Burbon Street about 3 a.m., where things were still jumping. The place never sleeps. I was happy to see Gene, and we had a good weekend on the town, but mentally I was a little displaced. Train travel just for fun does that to you. Think, about it. Get on the train in the desert at Phoenix, move along for a day or so without any contact with the outside world, then get off the train in bayou country.

Of course you see a lot of what passes by along the way, but you never touch it, never smell it or hear it. The window on the train is almost like a movie screen and you sit there in the audience wrapped up in your own romance with the rails. You can make the world that approaches and whips by and disappears do anything you want it to. The passing world stays where it is, but you keep movin' on down the line . . . looking . . . looking for that magic place that this train is carrying you to. You never quite get there, of course, but it's fun trying. I hope they never take the passenger trains away. I'll pay my share if that's what they want.

You need these little places to search for in life, some place that's not important to find, just a totally irrational, personal quest that you can head out on every now and then. I know, the reasoning is terrible, but forgive me. I still want to look for whatever it is that draws me off somewhere into the heatwaves where shimmering rails come together . . . and the red light at the back of the train wavers . . . blinks . . .

. . . and is gone.

Order from your book dealer or direct from publisher.

■■■■■■■■■■■■ *ORDER BLANK* ■■■■■

Golden West Publishers

4113 N. Longview Ave.,
Phoenix, AZ 85014

ON THE ARIZONA ROAD WITH BILL LEVERTON

Please ship the following books:

_____ Arizona Adventure ($5.00)

_____ Arizona Cook Book ($3.50)

_____ Arizona Hideaways ($4.50)

_____ Arizona Museums ($5.00)

_____ Arizona—Off the Beaten Path ($4.50)

_____ Arizona Outdoor Guide ($5.00)

_____ California Favorites Cook Book ($3.50)

_____ Chili-Lovers' Cook Book ($3.50)

_____ Citrus Recipes ($3.50)

_____ Cowboy Slang ($5.00)

_____ Explore Arizona ($5.00)

_____ Fools' Gold (Lost Dutchman Mine) ($5.00)

_____ Ghost Towns in Arizona ($4.50)

_____ Greater Phoenix Street Maps Book ($4.00)

_____ How to Succeed in Selling Real Estate ($3.50)

_____ In Old Arizona ($5.00)

_____ Mexican Cook Book ($5.00)

_____ On the Arizona Road ($5.00)

I enclose $ _____ (including $1 per order postage, handling).

Name _____

Address _____

City _____ State _____ Zip_____

This order blank may be photo copied

Books from Golden West Publishers

Read of the daring deeds and exploits of Wyatt Earp, Buckey O'Neill, the Rough Riders, Arizona Rangers, cowboys, Power brothers shootout, notorious Tom Horn, Pleasant Valley wars, "first" American revolution—action-packed true tales of early Arizona! *Arizona Adventure (by Marshall Trimble), 160 pages... $5.00.*

The lost hopes, the lost lives—the lost gold! Facts, myths and legends of the Lost Dutchman Gold Mine and the Superstition Mountains. Told by a geologist who was there! *Fools' Gold (by Robert Sikorsky), 144 pages . . . $5.00.*

Take the back roads to and thru Arizona's natural wonders—Canyon de Chelly, Wonderland of Rocks, Monument Valley, Rainbow Bridge, Four Peaks, Swift Trail, Alamo La' Virgin River Gorge, Palm Canyon, Red Ro Country! *Arizona—off the beaten path! (by Thelma Heatwole), 144 pages . . . $4.50.*

Plants, animals, rocks, minerals, geologic history, natural environments, landforms, resources, national forests and outdoor survival—with maps, photographs, drawings, charts, index. *Arizona Outdoor Guide (by Ernest E. Snyder), 126 pages . . . $5.00*

Visit the silver cities of Arizona's golden past with this prize-winning reporter-photographer. Come along to the towns whose heydays were once wild and wicked! See crumbling adobe walls, old mines, cemeteries, cabins and castles. *Ghost Towns and Historical Haunts in Arizona (by Thelma Heatwole), 144 pages . . . $4.50.*

Discover the Arizona that most tourists never see! Explore caves, ghost towns, ruins, lava tubes, ice caves, cliff dwellings! Sixty fabulous places, sixty full-page maps! *Explore Arizona! (by Rick Harris) 128 pages . . . $5.00.*

Index

Meet the author!

Bill Leverton is today a newsman who almost wasn't.

Fourteen years ago he quit the news business when it became too intense...giving him a glimpse of too much suffering he could do nothing about.

Bill gave journalism one more chance, this time at KTSP-TV, Channel 10 in Phoenix, where Leverton finally found his niche, writing the kind of stories he loves. People stories...places stories...about people and places almost anyone would like to know better.

Since then he has won many awards for both reporting and photography, including a dozen different first place awards in the Arizona Press Club and a Rocky Mountain Emmy where the competition includes journalists from all over the Southwest.

His first try at newspaper competition for his columns netted him a second-place award. The award went to his article called "Another Cowboy Gone"...the story of the passing of Frank Trammell, cowboy and well-known Arizona bluegrass harmonica player.

The competition judge praised Leverton for his "slow, even, easy style," and said the story was "perfectly adapted to its subject, and that is what feature writing is all about in my book."

The Trammell article is one of the chapters in Leverton's *On the Arizona Road with Bill Leverton.*

Born in Texas, raised mainly in New Mexico, he now calls Arizona home, with his stories reflecting his love of the Southwest.

A high school job as assistant to a portrait photographer first aroused the interest that eventually led to his now 23-year career as a photographer-reporter in television. He attended college in Texas and served in the U.S. Air Force.

Currently, Bill is writing a feature column, also called "On the Arizona Road," for several Arizona weekly newspapers, in addition to his television features for KTSP, Channel 10.

His busy schedule in television and writing leaves Leverton little time for his favorite hobbies of model railroading and aviation. He is a commercial fixed-wing and helicopter pilot.

His three grown children live in Arizona's Valley of the Sun. Bill and his wife Bonnie reside in Phoenix with their hybrid-wolf dog, Yukon Sam.